FINDING A WAY

FINDING A WAY

ESSAYS ON SPIRITUAL PRACTICE

Edited by Lorette Zirker

Charles E. Tuttle Co., Inc.
Boston • Rutland, Vermont • Tokyo

First published in 1996 by Charles E. Tuttle Co., Inc.
of Rutland, Vermont, and Tokyo, Japan, with editorial offices at
153 Milk Street, Boston, Massachusetts 02109.

Library of Congress Cataloging-in-Publication Data

Finding a Way : essays on spiritual practice / by Lorette Zirker, ed.
p. cm.
Includes bibliographical references.
ISBN 0-8048-3092-4
1. Spiritual life. I. Zirker, Lorette, 1930–
BL624.F516 1996   96–5156
291.4'4—dc20   CIP

First edition
1 3 5 7 9 10 8 6 4 2   05 04 03 02 01 00 99 98 97 96

Book design by Fahrenheit
Printed in the United States of America

This book
is dedicated
to all our teachers

TABLE OF CONTENTS

INTRODUCTION

THE THEME

We had a particular reason for putting together this book at this time.

Given the apparently insoluble problems we see in our country and in the world at this moment, many people turn to study, even if their sources are no more than their own experience and their own heads. We study history for the roots of these problems. We study sociology for explanations of the social upheavals we see in our streets and in the streets, deserts, mountains, and municipal squares of other people, as shown to us by agile photographers and unimaginable technology.

We try to figure out in our own minds what the world is coming to; why there are so many nasty changes from what we remember, or were told, of how life used to be lived not so long ago, whether those memories are accurate or not. What can we do about the anger and the greed, about the rigidities and the mental wall-building, and at the same time, the centrifugal explosions, that destroy civil life?

We have no choice but civil life. This planet requires it for its very continuation. Why then do so many people—leaders as well as followers—push and push for death—functional death, communal death, physical death?

How are we supposed to look at all this? Where is the viewing point from which we can see some kind of pattern? Can we see enough somehow to stop the disintegration? And further, what is it that moves us at least to ask these questions?

Some people react to the world with an instinct for survival that itself becomes part of the problem. We all know of those whose angry determination to save themselves from chaos, as they see it, raises the public blood pressure even higher. They blame, and they destroy. We especially know those moments in ourselves; sometimes we call them *being realistic*.

Some people will take shelter in rules—someone's rules, the more *sacred* the better—and will use their energies to force conformance to those rules by everyone else, in all spheres of life. By seeking to firm up a loose world, they run the risk of urging simplistic, rigid solutions for massively complex and jellylike problems. Eventually some of these people find themselves isolated and ignored, in small enclaves of *purity*, after having wrought untold damage to the very structures they were trying to sustain. Their works are not scary to begin with. Oh, how we long for simple rules. But then you hear a mother trying to control the ambiance of a local school, saying, "We believe in absolutes." Wait a minute, wait a minute—whose absolutes?

Then there are the bewildered but hopeful. They help the rest of us, for a moment or two. Sometimes we ought to plumb the depths of their hope. If there's more to it than mossy platitudes, it might be worth exploring.

Some people look for personal peace in the midst of external disorder and internal distraction. If I can find a quiet moment, I'll be able to think my way through to a way to live in this doomed age and then maybe help others survive. Don't they say Start with yourself? You can't change other people? Historic circumstances are what they are?

This desire is probably the beginning of sanity for all of us. If we have enough detachment to see this much, and if we can hang onto this detachment even if we become random victims, then maybe we unaggressive individuals may survive. There are a great many people who linger at this solution, thankful to be there. And this is the market for many bestsellers.

But there is yet another reaction to the ills of the earth and the anxiety within: that is to explore, and then choose, a path of understanding that eventually encompasses all levels of experience from the crudest to the most highly human. That way is a spiritual path, involving multidimensional inquiry that leads to a solid and satisfactory viewing point (and eventually, to different language and different views altogether). It offers the experiential equipment to cope with, and reduce, and help heal, those ills and those anxieties, wherever they are found. This inquiry takes one far deeper than the circumstances of the moment, whether sociological, historical, or personal. Its definition of *satisfying* has nothing at all in common with *comfort*. In fact, the relief it offers, and the remedial energy it stimulates, loses its private character completely.

The spiritual way, in its study and practice, is filled with ostensible paradoxes. It gives firm footing and straightforward direction, yet it wilts rigidities. It encourages determination yet abhors zeal. It demonstrates sure knowing while revealing layer after layer of not-knowing. It brings peace to the heart only after that personal heart is shown to be insubstantial. We will come to rest in the rhythmic beat of this way, but without being permitted to rest or retire into any half truths, cozy muddles, or unexamined delusions.

So this is a lifetime study. Or, as some would say, a study for life after life after life, without the usual concepts of comfort and relief, but with a new recognition of joy.

This book examines some of the traditional entranceways to the spiritual path and offers the taste and sound of their vocabularies, liturgies, and inner harmonies.

If you are having trouble with the word *spiritual* these days, it's no wonder. The word, I think, represents just a single need—the need for help and support in the midst of confusion and anxiety— but the help is sought through many definitions. I also think there is just a single characteristic we all hope for in this help—its quality of being more effective than we are. This includes its being more powerful than we are, more far-seeing and patient, and more broadly embracing. Although this need can be stated simply, let's not forget our own tendencies to swing from grand, planetary rea- sons for looking for this help to very personal and self-regarding reasons. And with this swinging go the various definitions of spiri- tuality.

Signs and symbols make up the meaning of spirituality for some. Important, for instance, may be certain objects, found in cer- tain locations, with their mythic or modern symbolic references. The connections and timing in events and sequences may be seen to be revealing. Some words and phrases seem to have the power to evoke what we call a spiritual feeling. This is part of our looking for, and hoping for, something sustaining and all-knowing just beyond our ken. Sometimes we accept what others say is powerful, and sometimes we make up our own rituals, declaring our own choice of objects and events as sacred, and we write our own litur- gies, in hope and sometimes in gratitude. But this probably is not a full meaning of spirituality; probably not a resting place.

Some people look for techniques. There must be some exercise (or sacrifice) devised by someone in some era that will open the doors of that just-beyond knowledge to me. There must be some- thing I can do. If I can do it, I'll know what spirituality is, and I can find peace and effect some change. Of course all the great traditions provide techniques and exercises as part of direction and training. They combine both preparation and sustenance, like a deep breath,

for a human body-mind that has to feel itself participating actively.
But neither is this the place to stop.

And there are those who need to take what might be called a scientific, or social-scientific, approach to spirituality. Begin with what we already know. What we think we know is quite a bit about the human personality. Look at the illnesses, societal and personal. Look at the way people function and fail to function as required. Infer the sources of the problems, both manifest (to others) and hidden (even to ourselves). Look at the sources that are statistically common and therefore somewhat predictable and describable. Look at those that seem to be unique or unpredictable, so far. Take a small leap and say that there certainly is a kind of *universality* pervading all these twistings and turnings. Be brave and take another leap, and begin to accept the evidence that most personalities actually recognize, and are pulled by, a sense of something more—something mysterious—something out there where health lies beyond illness and satisfaction beyond mute yearning. So let's, with valor, try to assess this Out There, as it relates to illness and behavior. Then let's talk about this and try to write about it, and we certainly will bring some relief and comfort to the public.

This particular attempt to respond to and to define spirituality, when tried all by itself, does not appeal to me at all. But it isn't a problem for some writers in this book, who see it more clearly than I do as a way station.

We all move back and forth through these definitions, these stages, these temporary places of rest, at different moments in our lives depending on our circumstances: a lit candle here, a prayerful recitation there, a self-imposed rigor here, an esoteric and sagacious nod there, a hopeful confidence placed in this one, a significance heard from that one. And we move up and down through different levels of understanding at each different moment. The fact remains that we know—we *know*—that these are partial definitions and partial solutions and resolutions of that continuing yearning toward comprehension and participation.

Although you will find references to, and descriptions of, these temporary sanctuaries throughout this book, you also will get a good look at what it might be like to continue, and continue, along a spiritual path, through heart's ease, and then the back of beyond, all the way to the next turn of a page, the slipping on of a shoe, the hug of someone helped, the untangling of a legislative knot, the washing of a dish. No more need for a resting place, and no more need for relief and comfort. Just continuance.

We talk about *exploring* in this book for at least two reasons. The first is that there are many vocabularies—many routes—from which to choose to pursue spiritual discovery. The second is that there are levels after levels that beckon and challenge.

A word here about choice and about challenge.

Perhaps it isn't accurate anymore to say that we're all born into, or brought up in, one of the major religious traditions. Maybe we aren't, and that can be good news or bad news. If you're a parent, it's worth at least a little thought. But if you yourself are drawn to spiritual questions at all, take some time with yourself and your books and a few elders—professed and lay—to find out which of the major traditions resonates best with you.

A tradition contains a depth of experience in study and in practice, and a supply of first-rate minds, which students need for a long time. Much as we like to assert our independent thinking, we find out sooner or later that we've wasted a lot of time with the hunt-and-peck method. There will be lots of time for independence and individuality, after a while, within a traditional direction. Perhaps my own essay will convince you of that.

A thorough grounding in one tradition—and *grounding* is the right word, and thoroughness is essential—will show us the universal in all traditions. We'll be able to speak more freely to one another on these matters, and gain more depth and width thereby. If we were brought up in one tradition but chose another more resonant one, we begin to see the same elements and the same universal inspiration in the former, underneath the phrases and images we

had rejected. Insights multiply. Differing historical backgrounds are
appreciated and given their proper weight. More quickly than
might be expected, we reach the point of seeing, and benefiting
from seeing, the difference between *religions* and *spirituality*. More
quickly then, we catch a glimpse of a time when both words may
simply drop off. In the essays to follow, you often will see the interplay between traditions, and the richness thereof.

Let's admit that there are those who, while deeply into their
traditions, do *not* see the underlying universality we in this book
see, along with numberless others. And history certainly provides us
with vivid contradictions to our thesis. The reasons for this profound difference of viewpoint—or viewing points—will be found in
the course of your own study and practice.

Exploring the choices of path, with mind and gut-resonator,
takes attention and decision. Exploring the challenges, the levels of
comprehension, takes some other faculties and some other factors
not always under our apparent control.

There is a sequence of levels of understanding, but that
sequence is not linear. We may think we will proceed steadily into
wisdom and compassion, but it's soon clear that we won't get our
wish, determined though we may be. There is an idiosyncratic and
unpredictable factor, for instance, that Eido Roshi has named The
Readiness of Time.

It works somewhat this way. You read a text in religion and
spirituality, and it must be in code. It's in English, but it doesn't get
past the eyes. It's supposed to be important, famous, profound, but
it's nonsense—the naked emperor of the desert or the mountain
cave. Forget it, you say, this is dumb. Literally. Five years later, that
something makes another appearance in your life, from another
source perhaps, in a different typeface, to a different you, and slam!
it's yours to have and to hold. There are endless variations on this
phenomenon.

This book presents many different levels of insight, some in the
same essay. Maybe *levels* isn't the right word; maybe onionskins

come into it. But challenge, exploration, and discovery are presented in these pages that have nothing to do with relief or comfort. They have nothing to do with euphoric glow (as Daido Loori elsewhere reminds us). At first glance, they don't seem to have much to do with personal virtue either—or with personal anything—or even with right and wrong, or good and evil. But they do offer a few openings into spiritual truth that the writers have discovered for themselves in the readiness of time. These openings have two sets of effects. They require a kind of personal adjustment of the mind and heart, a shifting to a new viewing point or to a new, more detailed map of the way. And they effect a new energy, a renewal to the challenge to experience greater human dimensions; energy to participate in the work beyond survival, the work of regeneration.

THE WRITERS

Who are the writers in this book, and what do they bring to it?

Ron Miller is a teacher. He brings to his teaching a long, deep, and continuous training in the scholarship and practice of religion and spirituality. When I first met him, he was wearing a collar and attending an interfaith meeting. He no longer wears a collar, but interfaith meetings of the mind are his life. To these years of study and dialogue, he has added the experience of a growing family. With these skills, he is well able to present the entranceways into the major spiritual traditions, along with some answers to what spiritual need is and why we feel it. I said earlier that studying and practicing one tradition enables you to begin to understand the wisdom in others. With a Jesuit grounding in Christianity, and with long biblical study, Miller was able to move into a comprehension of both the Old and the New Testaments that illuminates them for his students. His doctoral thesis was on the work of Franz Rosenzweig, a German thinker whose Jewish family were assimilated Christians but whose son began to rediscover his Jewish heritage. Rosenzweig eventually established a center for adult religious education at which he taught. With this in mind no doubt, Ron

Miller, a few friends, and a patron or two established a center for interfaith dialogue in the Chicago area. It is called Common Ground. It serves adults who come into it speaking different vocabularies but who leave its workshops and lectures able to translate particular religious concepts into a common spiritual language. They gain in appreciation, energy, and knowledge so as to pursue their own paths with encouragement and breadth. Miller is one of the most open-minded, equable people I know.

Beatrice Bruteau offers a great challenge, to me and to many readers. Her language and imagery move in and out of the New and Old Testaments with an unexpected flavor that we name these days Eastern and esoteric. That's not so surprising when you learn that her original interest was in the study of Hindu Vedanta and that she was a student of Dom Bede Griffiths, the Catholic monk who founded a center for Hindu-Christian study in India. Bruteau is a prolific writer of books and articles who also gives workshops and lectures. She and her partner, James Somerville, are most active with professed and lay contemplative students of many traditions. She is currently directing the training and development of a new kind of lay order for men and women who are Christian contemplatives in the midst of the everyday world. Because of her cheerful, insistent exhortations (at least that's the way I hear them) to read more widely, to practice harder, and to probe more deeply, I find, translating rapidly as I go, my Buddhist difficulties and inner resistances simply melting in the heat. I only wish I understood all that she understands of human and universal truth. How much more effective manifestations we might be if we were able to integrate more of her insights into ourselves, and ourselves into the Whole.

In **Annabeth McCorkle's** essay we find that strange yearning we all feel made more substantial. She sees it as an "inner imperative." She then makes more visible the materials of spiritual practice with which we work, particularly the practice of Attention. And she makes more vivid the "shift of perspective" or change of viewing point that is the continuing goal of the student. McCorkle was raised in a Protestant family, and her reading in Christianity still continues. As an adult, she began her deeper spiritual studies with practice in the Gurdjieff work. Then there came a concentrated period of Zen Buddhist study with Roshi Kapleau. After this, she returned to, and has continued for more than thirty years in, the Gurdjieff work. With their families now grown, McCorkle and her husband continue to offer their guidance to students.

For **Laura Bernstein,** the readiness of time brought a surge of interest in spirituality and eventually in Judaism. Along with this growing interest and experience, a number of opportunities arose. She studied Buddhism for a period. She attended workshops at Common Ground. She became interested in mysticism and Kabbalah. She was also raising a family. Bernstein began, with the inspiration of Ron Miller and Rabbi Douglas Goldhamer, to see in Judaism the wisdom-tradition of great depth that she had not seen in childhood. She wanted to know very well—to become expert in—a single tradition. Exploring spirituality in the context of Judaism and its history, she found to her own astonishment the desire to be "a learned Jew." In her essay here, we can read about some of that exploration and become more familiar with that vocabulary.

The usage of the word *enlightenment* has broadened considerably since my first Zen meeting almost thirty years ago. It has been adapted to very different circumstances to express many conditions. However, **Judith Blackstone,** in her essay here, stays within the customary meaning as she offers a physical and an emotional as well as a spiritual description of enlightenment as she has seen it and felt it. The word has been connected most closely with the principal shift of viewing point in the course of spiritual study. Blackstone calls it "realizing fundamental consciousness." Her own vocabulary is very clear and comes from study and practice in Buddhism and Hindu Vedanta. She has gone on to develop and teach what she titles in her books and workshops Subtle Self Work, continuing her exploration into the maturing self and its spiritual goal.

What is this Whole I mentioned? **Robert Granat** writes of this in his essay. He gives us, in all his many writings, some sense of the larger picture, the more integrated view, of what we're trying to learn about. Although born into a Jewish family, Granat is more comfortable with Buddhist and Christian vocabularies. He translates freely between them, using his literary skills to try to convey the unity, or fusion, of the individual in the universe. Both Granat and his wife have studied in several traditions, finding their teachers among the wise in each. Sometimes they are able to meet their teachers in person. At other times they make use of books, tapes, correspondence, and of course their own practice. Neither the distractions of family nor the stresses of geography are an impediment to developing one's spiritual insight. In fact . . .

My own contribution to this book is an informal recounting of some of my adventures with spiritual practice. The mystery is how I ever came to be drawn to this subject at all. My family is nonobservant Jewish, very much political and social activist rather than inclined toward spirituality. My academic studies were in politics and economics, and my friends were of mixed faiths, none of them Eastern. Even my decades-long friendship with Annabeth McCorkle began years before our formal interest in these matters took shape. Why then did Zen Buddhism boom so loudly, so it seemed, for my attention? Here is a second mystery. But Zen showed itself definitely to be my vocabulary, and I have been finding my way in it ever since. And by its means, I've been able to see into Judaism much more deeply than before and to appreciate Catholic and Jewish language, metaphor, and wisdom. Although there is little mention in my essay of zazen, chanting, bowing, or other traditional Zen practices, be assured that rigorous, and strenuous, monastic training underlies my informality. My husband was an unfailing support in all this study, especially when the family was young, and his understanding, which still underlies our friendship, has paralleled mine.

AND SO . . .

We are looking especially at *renewal* in this book, particularly renewal of practice. There is a luxurious growth of "explanation" these days; there is also much description, both of our own ills and society's. We want to believe that if we can describe a malady minutely enough, and explain it precisely enough, the cure will become obvious. But I think the cures we need today will become obvious only to those who experience in themselves the radical shift of perspective we've been talking about. We must alert ourselves to prepare for these experiences and for the transformations that begin before them and that follow them. We will need to make a devoted effort in study, practice, and simple digestion and absorption. We also will need a kind of timeless patience. And we will need to recognize the intimations that perhaps this effort is not being made *for* ourselves or *by* ourselves. Zen Buddhists have an expression: "returning to the marketplace with bliss-bestowing hands."

What peace is that, and what is bestowing it?

—Lorette Zirker
Mountain Park, New Mexico

FINDING A WAY

SPACE FOR SPIRIT

Ron Miller

INTRODUCTION

Space for Spirit

Our society seems so often spiritless, crabbed and cramped in its materialistic wrappings. Many of us find ourselves longing to recover spirit in our workplace and indeed in all aspects of our living space. We thirst to sink our roots down into what the fourteenth-century German mystic, Meister Eckhart, referred to as a divine river, coursing clear, underneath our arid and superficially surfaced world; into those depths that the poet-priest Gerard Manley Hopkins called "the dearest freshness deep down things." We recognize all too clearly the pervading malady, the "loss of soul" that Thomas Moore describes so well in his deservedly popular *Care of the Soul*. We seek room to stretch, and space for spirit.

I once saw the world in terms of a battle being waged. When I was a young Jesuit seminarian, I saw the battle as between the truth of Roman Catholic Christianity and all other forms of half-truth or total error. Even when still a high school student at a Jesuit school, I can remember how lustily we sang of the "earth's battlefield" where this spiritual warfare was being carried on.

It is now more than twenty years since I left the Jesuits, and I still see the world as a battlefield sometimes, but the battle I recognize today is not one being fought for Catholicism or Judaism or Buddhism or for any other of the competing "-isms" of our ideological landscape. It is rather a battle for spirit, for an alternative to a numbing and reductionistic secular culture. Spirit has indeed been sucked from our socialized world and we are gasping for that breath God once puffed into Adam's clay; we are seeking some breeze of that holy spirit that once moved so mightily over creation's waters. Like the deer of Psalm 42, thirsting for running water, so do our souls thirst for living spirit.

A Context for Dialogue

Towards the end of Rabbi Harold Kushner's latest book *To Life! A Celebration of Jewish Being and Thinking,* he talks about a congregant chiding him for the fact that he was going to visit a Christian church where he would be speaking "for the competition." But he responds that Christianity is not the competition; apathy, selfishness, and all that denies the transcendent in our nature and our life—they are the competition. He concludes by saying that the church and the synagogue are allies; they are on the same side of the battle. No words could better express my own feelings on the matter. Spiritual paths should not be seen in competition but rather as spokes in the same wheel, leading to the same hub, the same reality of spirit.

Andrew Harvey makes the same point in his book *The Way of Passion,* an enthusiastic introduction to the mystical poetry of the great Sufi Jalal al-Din, popularly known as Rumi. Harvey quotes one of Rumi's poems where he asserts that he is neither Christian nor Jew, not a Zoroastrian nor even a Muslim. He proclaims himself rather to be in "astounding lucid confusion" and asks us not to nail him down in a box of cold words. Harvey uses this line as a springboard to his own assertion that we should not be trapped in our various religious identities. For we are really "using a particular sacred way to get to the placeless, the nameless, and the wayless." We should be using the "sacred technology" that speaks to us but not be caught in labels. Again, like Rabbi Kushner, Harvey urges us to respect all those other sacred ways that lead our fellow human beings to the wells of spirit. They are our allies, not our enemies.

More than twenty years ago now, I was involved in the founding of Common Ground, an organization for interfaith study and dialogue. Like Kushner and Harvey, those of us who stood at its beginning saw the great spiritual traditions as allies, not as competitors. I remember a discussion I once had with an Evangelical Christian minister who stated that we could at least share the premise that if one religion were true, then all the others were false. I answered (and it was an answer I had first heard from a longtime friend and colleague of mine, Jim Kenney) that my starting point would rather be that if one religion were true, there's a good chance that they all are. Years of studying diverse religious paths has deepened this conviction for me.

Mystery

It was sometime in the sixth grade. Sister Stephanie was teaching us how to calculate the area of the room for laying a hypothetical carpet. I was looking out the window, realizing how uninterested I was in the problem, when she ended the mathematics lesson and began the religion segment of our day. I remember her asking me to open all the windows. I complied, although it was a wintry day, as she announced that we would all need fresh air because we were going to be discussing a mystery so deep that no one could understand it. We were going to be talking about the Trinity, how God could be both one and three. She immediately captured my interest; here was something that could never be answered. This was something to whet my appetite.

This peculiar fascination of mine for questions without answers has influenced my choice of major areas of concentration ever since. I have always been drawn to languages and translation, where one soon recognizes the truth of the Italian proverb that every translator is necessarily a traitor (*traduttore, traditore*). Then I was led to a graduate degree in philosophy, nothing along the line of the linguistic analysts or logicians, but to the classical philosophers and the later existentialists. In philosophy, all the major questions are recycled, asked again in every age but never definitely answered. Finally, my doctoral work led me to the study of comparative religions, another area where truths are transrational, beyond the methods of rational analysis and conversion to mathematical symbols. I have sedulously avoided all areas of study where clear and definite answers are the norm.

It was Gabriel Marcel (1889–1973), the French existentialist philosopher and playwright, whose writings articulated for me what I had obscurely felt since that distant day in the sixth-grade classroom. It was from him that I first learned the crucial distinction between a problem and a mystery. A problem is something that has a solution because it is presented to us as something within limits, that is, defined. *Finis*, the basic Latin root of *defined*, as well as *finish* and *finite*, means any kind of boundary, border, or limit. A problem, in other words, revolves around something that can be defined or objectified. But an object, in terms of its Latin roots, is something "thrown against us"; in German, an object is a *Gegenstand*, literally something that "stands over against" us. So problems and objects both tend to separate us from something. The business with the carpet and the area of the room was, of course, a classic problem. A problem entails something I can separate myself from, place over against me, put under a microscope, hang on the wall, objectify, delimit, keep at a distance.

A mystery, on the other hand, is not reducible to being a problem. It is not something over against me but something that contains me, not an object separable from me but a context within which I find myself. It is something of which I will never have an adequate definition. I am not in front of a mystery but inside it. A mystery, therefore, in principle cannot be solved. Death, life, God, freedom, good, evil, friendship, love—all of these turn out to be mysteries. Can I separate myself, for example, from death? Of course not. As Heidegger reminds us, our very being is a "*Sein zum Tode*," a "being towards death." We have no way of understanding ourselves outside of that horizonal reality of our dying. Death simply cannot become an object; and the same is true for the other mysteries. In fact, nothing really important can be defined or isolated. My boyhood instinct was right. The Trinity really was something quite different from the area of the room.

What then is the proper response to a mystery? Participation. It's the same word in Marcel's original French and in English. One doesn't solve a mystery; one participates in it. The mystery is not totally unknowable, living in some morass of mere feelings where no light of knowledge can penetrate. Marcel asserts an immediate participation, what he sometimes calls a "blinded intuition," but this is accompanied by a conceptual process as well as by such allied virtues as love and fidelity.

Participation is an interesting alternative to solution. The word somehow conjures up the image of lowering oneself into a hot tub. As a whole person, not as a disembodied intellect, we come to know the mystery in which we participate. And this participation is not a single act but a process, often a lifetime of loving and faithful involvement and commitment. Again we see the significance of Marcel's understanding of "creative fidelity."

It's difficult to express adequately how much this freed up my life as an undergraduate seminarian. Caught in the demands of a rationalistic system, I saw a place towards which I could move, a future towards which I could strive. Truth wasn't something to be neatly packaged and memorized, bound by linear thought and argumentation. There was an aspect of knowing and connectedness with reality that was consonant with what I had long ago intuited. So much was mystery, everything worthwhile really, and even though it could not be solved, it could be explored through participation. That made all the difference. It gave my spirit space to breathe and move, even run. The understanding of mystery and the approach to it through participation became absolutely fundamental to my further explorations.

The Holy

What is the particular mystery that underlies our spiritual journeys? Rudolf Otto (1869–1937), the great student of world religions, helped me here with his attention to the category of holiness. The title of his classic work, *Das Heilige*, was poorly translated into English as *The Idea of the Holy*. "The holy" is not an idea but a primordial category of experience, and the work would be better titled through a more exact translation of the German as simply *The Holy*. In studying the sacred literature of countless religions, Otto found a primary experience that was not reducible to any other category. It was an experience of the numinous, the holy, and it involved an ambivalent response on the part of human beings that led Otto to use the Latin phrase *"mysterium tremendum et fascinans"*—a mystery at once both overwhelming and attractive.

What is described in chapter six of the Book of Isaiah as the prophet's temple vision, where he is both drawn to the holy presence and simultaneously repelled by his own sense of sinfulness, and what is attributed to Peter in the fifth chapter of Luke's gospel, when Peter asks Jesus to depart from him since he is a sinner—this very ambivalence of feeling is seen by Otto as characteristic of our awareness of the holy. We are drawn to it, recognizing here that very depth for which our souls have longed, and yet we are overwhelmed by a mystery so immense, so pure, so wholly other. We encounter here the legitimate "fear of the Lord"; not the servile cringing of the slave before the master, but standing in awe (what Rabbi Abraham Joshua Heschel called "radical amazement") before this mystery that is at once so overwhelming and yet so compelling. These are moments that lead us to take off our shoes, like Moses in the third chapter of the Book of Exodus, when he encounters the bush that burns without being consumed.

In addition to teaching in the Religion Department at Lake Forest College, I am the faculty coordinator of our Interfaith Center. Some years ago, we were given a space allowing us to have a room for meditation. One of the first things the students mandated was that this was to be an area where you must take your shoes off. They added elements of incense, rugs, and wall hangings. I stood in fascination as I watched this group of students reinvent the accoutrements of sacred space. It was as if they had all come fresh from reading the works of Rudolf Otto and Mircea Eliade—which was definitely not the case.

In her thoughtful book *Encountering God*, Harvard's Diana Eck talks about a Christian missionary among the Hindus who asked his fellow missionaries, in 1938, whether they sometimes met a religious faith that was not Christian but was nevertheless a faith, in the approach to which "one ought to put the shoes off the feet." What a marvelous expression and what a profound recognition of that primordial awareness of the numinous. Other missionaries have surely sensed now and again the mystery of the holy in those they were trying to "convert." And those undergraduates who were furnishing a meditation room intuitively knew that they were setting up a space where something could be encountered that could lead us to put the shoes off the feet.

The Door Is Everywhere

Where is the place of such encounters? Where is the door to the mystery where holiness dwells? This is a question that most spiritual traditions would invert. Where could there *not* be a place for such encounters? What particle of experience could *not* serve as such a door? The German Jesuit theologian Karl Rahner once said that if there is indeed a God, then nothing could truly be godless, not even the experience of the atheist. Perhaps this is what the greatest of medieval thinkers, Thomas Aquinas, meant when he said that everything that exists participates in the divine reality by the very fact that it exists; he went on to add that this even applies to Satan and his minions. Psalm 139 gave expression to this insight centuries ago when the psalmist asked, "Whither shall I go from thy spirit? or whither shall I flee from thy presence? If I ascend up into heaven, thou art there; if I make my bed in hell, behold, thou art there."

Avery Dulles was a young atheist in college when the sight of the "new green" of springtime propelled him into an awareness of the Creator. Today he is a Jesuit theologian and scholar. Whitaker Chambers, author of *The Witness*, saw his atheism dissolve into faith while watching the oatmeal drip from the ear of his baby daughter. Could such a delicate instrument as that ear be nothing more than a chance concatenation of atoms? Suddenly the divine was present in a worldview that had earlier found no room for God. The new green of spring and the intricacy of a baby's ear became occasions for taking off the shoes.

If such simple events can constitute a miracle, then what could *not* be a miracle for one with eyes to see and ears to hear? A miracle is not an unusual event but an event to which we are led to pay unusual attention. And that possibility of exquisite attention lives in every moment and in every event. I knew a woman who told me that she never felt more in touch with the divine than when she was digging around her rosebushes. She said that this is why she liked the phrase used so often by that giant of Protestant theology, Paul Tillich, for it was Tillich who referred to God as "the Ground of Being." And how many fathers like myself would testify that watching the birth of their children was a numinous moment of the first order? Even experienced medical personnel often find tears in their eyes in those moments, recognizing somehow what the great philosopher and religious thinker, Martin Buber, meant when he said that the birth of a child recapitulates the very mystery of creation itself.

If the door is everywhere, all that is wanting is our attentiveness. I will be talking about attentiveness later in this essay, and it suffices for now simply to point to its crucial significance. Years of teaching the Bible have alerted me to the centrality of having one's eyes and ears open, looking and listening for the divine word. In Deuteronomy 29:4, Moses complains about those who have neither eyes to see nor ears to hear, and this same lament is found in Jeremiah 5:21: "Hear this, O foolish and senseless people, who have eyes, but do not see, who have ears, but do not hear." Psalm 40, verse 4, sings of the gratitude of one who has been given "an open ear." The English word *obey* itself, so common in the language of spiritual practice, comes from the Latin root words *ob* and *audire*, to hear carefully; in much the same way, the German word *gehorchen* (to obey) comes from *horchen* (to listen). All messages fail when there is no receiver.

PARTICIPATION

Grace, Faith, and Works

Before proceeding any further toward participation, it might make sense to try to clarify some concepts that have generated heated polemics in some circles—not only Christian, but Buddhist as well—for no small number of centuries. Was Martin Luther right with his battle cry: "*Sola gratia; sola fides; sola scriptura!*"— "Grace alone; faith alone; scripture alone!"? Such exclusivity of language is almost guaranteed to miss the mark, at least if one approaches the divine with the expectation that paradox usually comes the closest to overcoming the inadequacy of human language.

I would attempt a nuance of Luther's language a bit. (Luther wasn't always at his best with nuances.) From one perspective, everything is God's gift. From one perspective, the whole spiritual path is a response of faith or trust on our part. From one perspective, the canonical scriptures must provide the norm and corrective for the aberrations of the earthly representatives of a tradition. And yet, from another prespective, no gift of grace is adequately understood without attention to the act whereby it is received. So too, no faith or trust is complete without its overflow into good works. And scripture, too, consists of books belonging to the community that proclaims them, and their interpretation is inherent in their every use. There is, in other words, despite the most fervent hopes of fundamentalists of every stripe, no uninterpreted scripture.

Nevertheless, Luther is undoubtedly right to remind the people of his time, and of our time as well, that the initiative always belongs to the divine and that the human component is always a response. To recognize that divinely offered gift (grace) and to trust that gift and its giver (faith) seem self-evidently primordial to any spiritual path. How much ink has been wasted in the misplaced battle between grace/faith and good works? Why do we get caught so often on false dilemmas and unnecessary dualities? No choice has to be made between faith and good works. They live together as naturally as our breathing in and breathing out. Indeed our intake of breath is a beautiful symbol of faith in the divine gift of life, and our breathing out is a trustful giving of ourselves to the service of others until our last breath is spent.

All the great traditions recognize the priority of the divine gift, of grace, and of the need to trust life in the direction of that gift and its giver. The giving of the revelation at Sinai is referred to in the Jewish tradition as *matan torah*—the gift of the Torah. The Torah is Israel's "grace," and a Jewish life of good works is a grateful response to such a great gift. Buddha didn't wrench enlightenment from heaven under the Bo tree; he received it. The Tao cannot be manipulated into existence, nor could the Quran have been forced from Allah by Muhammad. Grace always comes first, and faith lies inevitably in the most fundamental order of response.

A marvelously illustrative story of this basic truth is found in the synoptic gospels (Mark 10, Matthew 19, Luke 18). A certain man (Matthew identifies him as a young man, and Luke calls him a ruler) approaches Jesus and asks what he must do to have eternal life. What is striking here is identical in all three versions. The young man presumes that the initiative is his to take. Perhaps this stems from his being rich; we are told later that he has many possessions. (Luke simply states straight out that "he was very rich.") It's an important detail. He exhibits what we today might call a "consumer mentality." He tends to see life in terms of possessions. Money can indeed buy anything. Everything has its price. Why not see eternal life that way too? What does he have to do to acquire it? How can he add eternal life to his other possessions?

This is precisely the attitude that contradicts the reality of grace, and it presents quite a challenge to Jesus as a spiritual teacher. How does he deal with the challenge? Jesus leads the young man into a consideration of the commandments. After all, fulfilling the commandments is a grateful response to the God who revealed them, and obeying the commandments is without question a way that leads to life. When the young man asks Jesus which commandments he has in mind, Jesus lists those having to do with one's fellow human beings. The very youth of this young man might well be revealed by his somewhat glib answer, that he has been keeping those commandments since he was a child. There's a certain smugness in presuming that the commandments are so easily kept.

Perhaps it was Jesus' recognition of all the problems emerging in this brief exchange that led him to make "an end run." It seems to me that Jesus sees this man as so immured in his control systems and his consumer obsessions that he decides to leave the issue of the commandments and directly attack the grace-denying consciousness that lies at the root of the man's problems. Skilled reader of souls that he is, Jesus sees that the issue of possessing things is what's blocking any kind of spiritual life in this man. Jesus' words, "Sell your possessions and give the money to the poor," must have hit that young man like an explosion. It was an all-or-nothing dare on Jesus' part. He knew that he would have to dislodge that whole way of thinking or achieve nothing that day.

The latter seems to have been the case as the young man goes away "sad, because he had many possessions." He was not ready that day for the reality of grace or for the trusting act of faith. He failed to see that one can enter the mystery of the holy only with grace and gratitude, not with an attitude of control or manipulation.

That refusal on the young man's part leads naturally to a consideration of faith. He failed, after all, to trust the invitation of Jesus. Biblical faith is not something living above the eyebrows. It is not "belief about" something, expressed in a creedal formulation or dogmatic proposition. Faith is essentially trust. It is the way we trust our lives forward. Faith is the way we open ourselves to the future. The Hebrew word *emunah* is from the same root as *amen*. When Jews or Christians end a prayer or song with their amen, they are saying in effect that the words expressed are worthy of trust, that they are the kind of words they can rely on, the kind of words that will open them to an authentic future, the kind of words upon which they can build their lives.

What we trust underlies every action in each moment of our life. When we step into an elevator, we are trusting the mechanism that operates it. When we breathe air, we are trusting that its chemical composition is consistent with our basic survival. When we take a job for its salary rather than for its "fit" with our own interests and inclinations, we are trusting the saving power of money. Life really doesn't offer us the option of having faith or not having faith. It's rather a matter of which faith we will have, what we will finally trust. Even commiting suicide implies a trust that one's condition afterwards will be better than the present one, although it seems uncertain who will be there to enjoy the improvement.

Grace, then, is first on God's part, in almost any portrayal of the spiritual life. Faith is first on the human part. As we see, how one trusts one's life forward precedes every choice we make. What about good works? They flow quite naturally from God's grace and our faith. Recognizing the gift with grateful hearts, and trusting the gift with the whole dynamic of our existence, we move readily to the good works that follow.

This brings us naturally into the realm of practice. We now see that practice is not some sort of effort to lift oneself up spiritually by one's own bootstraps.

Gurus, Teachers, Directors

In thinking about practice, many people are first inclined to find a teacher. This makes a good deal of sense. I remember once attending a talk by Karen Armstrong (author of *A History of God* and several other excellent books). At the end of the presentation, a woman in the audience talked very personally about her own confusion and asked Karen where and how she should begin her search. I was interested in how Karen was going to answer this. The other questions had all been factual ones, which she could handle easily. Here was a more existential question, a real cry for help. Karen thought for a moment and then pointed out that since she didn't live in this area, she wasn't aware of all the resources here, but she suggested that the young woman ask around and find someone who is wise.

Find someone who is wise. That's a marvelous answer. Someone with wisdom can help us on our own path. But what is wisdom and how does it differ from mere knowledge, or from the acquisition of information, with which our culture is so enamored? Thomas Aquinas says of wisdom that it "judges all things and orders them because it looks at matters in terms of their highest causes." It seems then that the primary characteristic of wisdom is this function of ordering. What use is a stockpile of information if there is no one who can put it in some kind of order? That's the real gift of the wise person, the ability to see things in relationship, in terms of a larger picture or pattern. A little wisdom at the beginning of one's path goes a long way.

Must such a wise person be a human being currently on this planet? That may sound like a strange question, but when Thomas Merton, one of the great spiritual guides of our century, met with the Tibetan Buddhists, they referred to this Christian monk as a Jesus lama. In other words, from their perspective, his truest teacher was Jesus, alive and present in the community of faith. Can a Christian today then claim Jesus as teacher and guide? By the same token, Moses continues to teach through Torah and Talmud and on through the latest utterance of Jewish wisdom. A rabbinic story goes so far as to assert that Moses heard on Sinai everything that would be Torah-teaching to the end of human history. Can a Jew today still claim Moses as teacher and guide? I think the answer to both these questions is a resounding yes.

Must the teacher be a person at all? What about a book? *The Urantia Book*, for example, is studied by its followers as an authentic revelation, but without any known connection to a particular human being as vehicle of that revelation. Others would find a guide in *The Course in Miracles* or any of the numerous books offering spiritual guidance available to us today. One could well turn to a book like Jack Kornfield's *A Path with Heart* and find a wise guide on the spiritual path. Or one could follow the path laid out by Thomas Moore through his many writings. And that holds true for many another useful, spiritual vade mecum. I will speak later of the particular form of yoga or spiritual practice that finds an anchoring in a sacred text.

Regarding the guidance of books, however, as well as teachers not available in our ordinary world of experience, I would venture one caveat: The possibility of dialogue is limited in these situations. The book can't respond to the question or objection you're formulating in this moment. Nor, except to some remarkable mystics, do Jesus or Moses respond to the pressing exigency of the searcher. It is for this reason, I believe, that Karen Armstrong wanted the questioner to have some contact with an available source of wisdom, one who can readily be addressed and spoken to in the here and now. There is, in other words, something to be said for the living teacher.

Having said that, let's remember that the scandal sheets have been packed with news about Catholic priests, Buddhist masters, Hindu gurus, televangelists, and teachers of every persuasion who have used their office to exploit their followers. The stories vary, but sex and money are the predominant themes, two powerful forces to tempt even the enlightened. Perhaps this is the moment to remind ourselves of the teaching of Shunryu Suzuki that, in the strict sense, only behavior is enlightened, not persons. Jack Kornfield gives some helpful guidelines in the book I mentioned earlier. He asks us to avoid what he calls "the halo effect." He means the assumption that if a teacher exhibits wisdom or enlightened activity in one area, we are correct in presuming that this teacher is enlightened in all of his or her activities.

People who claim enlightenment merit suspicion. We need to be cautious consumers in the spiritual supermarket of our society. There's some strong advice to this effect in Stephen Butterfield's *The Double Mirror*, which has as its subtitle *A Skeptical Journey into Buddhist Tantra*. He faces, head-on, matters of scandal and controversy, and his message is Be Discerning! Butterfield analyzes some of the practices that contribute to the corruption of our teachers. And I remember the adage that when you become a bishop, you will never eat a bad meal, or hear the truth, again.

I am encouraged by the emergence today of another type of spiritual direction. It is called peer direction or spiritual friendship. While recognizing the need for feedback and dialogue with someone who is wise, I see that these new relationships foster mutuality, constructive criticism, and healthy doubt. I tend to eschew the model of the exalted master, protected from challenge and critique. I prefer the spiritual friend or peer director who sits on the same level with me, recognizing that we are both on the journey, that we must both discern the path of wisdom, the enlightened activity, the compassionate deed. I believe that this allows us to find the guidance we need, but protects us from the abuses that appear all too readily, even in the holiest of places.

Attention

As I noted earlier, the door to the mystery of holiness, the door to true practice, the door opening on the path, is found wherever there is attentiveness. The disciple who climbs the Himalayas asks the master for the most important principle of enlightened living. "Attention" is the answer. "What about the second most important principle?" queries the exhausted climber. "Attention," responds the master in a louder voice. "And the third most important principle?" the seeker pleads. "Attention," the master booms in reply. Was it really worth his climb to learn something so seemingly innocuous? Yes, it is worth any effort to discover the key to the door of true practice.

I wonder if I sound as if I'm trivializing spiritual traditions by saying that a great deal of what they're about has to do with getting our attention. Some things—like excruciating pain, and the proximity of death—are natural attention-grabbers. And yet, wouldn't it be helpful to wake up before we die? Natalie Goldberg, in the introduction to her wonderful book *Long Quiet Highway: Waking Up in America*, tells us that this is the real purpose of her book, learning to wake up before we die. Don't we all agree that it would be better to find our life before it's over? But it's interesting how these two realities are brought together in spiritual teaching—that is, learning to live before we die implies learning to die before it's time to die. In other words, learning to die and learning to live seem inextricably linked in the great spiritual traditions. Attention to one implies attention to the other as well.

Martin Buber's life was changed by an indirect contact with death. He had begun his day well, enjoyed a peaceful meditation, and was just getting down to the business of the day when a student came to see him. In retrospect, he felt he was polite with the student and answered the questions he was asked, but at the same time he may well have communicated the fact that this was something of an interruption in his otherwise peaceful morning. The student left, and a few days later Buber learned that this young man had committed suicide. Buber never forgot that tragedy. He understood himself as having heard the words the student spoke but as having neglected the unspoken words, the silent plea for help of this human being who came to him at a time of direst need. From then on, Buber was determined to have no other religion than the moment, with its possibility for dialogue. What can one exchange, after all, for the reality of this moment? What future riches or delight can be promised in exchange for the one thing that is real and present?

One of the first prayers any Catholic Christian learns is the Hail Mary. It ends with the petition: "Pray for us now and at the hour of our death." I have often reflected on the spiritual wisdom of that plea. In all the diversity of our lived experience, there are only two moments of which we are certain: the present moment and the moment of our death. One day these two will coincide. If we need spiritual help, these are the two most appropriate places to direct the energies of the universe. Spiritual traditions inevitably focus on these two moments: the moment at hand, this irreplaceable opportunity, and the moment of our death.

Paul Tillich developed a theology around the opportune character of the present moment. He noted that the Greek language, the language of the Christian Testament, has two words for time: *chronos*, which refers to the kind of time measured by the clock, and *kairos*, which refers to a moment of time as filled with opportunity. When we say it's noon, we are speaking of chronological time. But when the midwife tells us it's time now for the woman to deliver her baby, this is kairotic time. Kairotic time is the time of blossoms bursting open in spring, of fruit ripening on the vines, and of the birthing of everything new.

Kairotic time is also the time of repentance. My students are used to seeing me draw a large circle on the board to represent the divine and then a small circle, outside the perimeter of the large circle, to represent our anemic and neurotic ego. The Hebrew word for repentance is *teshuvah*, "turning"; this same root idea of turning is in the English word *conversion*. Repentance entails the movement from an eccentric existence in which we move centrifugally (fleeing the center), to a concentric existence in which we move centripetally (seeking the center), toward that point in which our self-identity and the divine identity are one. From the biblical perspective, this movement characterizes a person as *zaddik*, "righteous," in a right relation with God, God-centered. Attention to the moment as opportune for turning to the divine center is in some sense the essence of biblical spirituality.

There is much debate about how we are to understand biblical language about the end of human history. Here too I find much help in Tillich's insight. Just as the next moment is the moment of death—that is, there are no certain moments between this one and the moment of death—so too the next cosmic moment is the end of the universe's history. For there too no certain moment can be relied on between now and the hour of the death of the cosmos. Living attentively thus means living just one moment from the end, that is, from the end of our own life and from the end of the life of the cosmos as well. A wide-eyed alertness characterizes this existentially attentive lifestyle. It means living every moment as a plunge into space with only the secured bungee cord of this moment as anchor.

I learned the meaning of this wide-eyed alertness through a man who became a dear friend at the end of his life. He had come back from the hospital that spring to spend his last days at home. He was cancer-ridden and filled with pain, but he graciously made a space for me in his life. We would meet for a few minutes each day, whenever the pain was controlled enough by the medication that he could have a visitor. I remember him telling me once that sometimes when he first woke up in the morning, there was a fleeting second or two when he would hear the song of a bird or see the sunlight playing on the wallpaper of his bedroom. Then the first stabbing pain would strike and he would be instantly thrown back into the reality of his imminent death. Nevertheless, he told me, those precious seconds were worth the days of pain. I knew immediately that if I could begin to cherish each moment of my life that way, I would have learned the lesson of attention.

Lectio Divina

When Saint Benedict, the sixth-century father of Western monasticism, wrote his rule, he saw a monk's life divided between manual work (about five hours), prayer (both private and communal), and the *lectio divina*, literally the "divine or sacred reading." I find it rendered "prayerful reading" in a modern translation of the rule, and that seems to catch the meaning of what Benedict wants to say. This prayerful reading is one of the tactics to be used by a monk against that idleness which is the enemy of the soul. I spoke earlier about the fact that the door to the mystery is everywhere, but I would like to expand on this idea of the *lectio divina* as one door to the mystery of the holy that has proved helpful to me.

Yoga comes from the same root as our word *yoke*, and there are certainly many ways to be yoked to the divine. To use a particular yoga is to be a yogi of that practice. Some people are drawn by the emotional intensity of devotional yoga, while others have been attracted to the yoga of action in the world. Sometimes we find that several yogic strands are woven together in a person's life and practice. That has been my own personal experience too; and yet it is the yoga of study that I especially cherish. I may be part of that dying breed of book people, those who are drawn to the written text as their natural habitat. Any of the places I nest in are feathered with books–my office, my end of the sofa at home, the nightstand on my side of the bed. I am a reading addict, and religious texts have a special significance for me.

A sacred text is a holy gate. It is even worth the effort to learn a new language to enter such a gate. One can't fully absorb the world of the Hebrew Bible without the Hebrew language. The rabbinic commentaries sometimes focus on the very shape of the Hebrew letter, like the initial *bet* with which Genesis begins. The Christian Testament was nowhere more alive to me than when I heard the gospel chanted in the original Greek in a darkened monastery chapel on the lovely island of Patmos. Greek is a language I have studied since my high school days, and I memorized the cadences of the opening lines of John's gospel long before I knew their theological content. My summer project is to learn enough Arabic to sound the words of the Quran, since the English interpretations of the text seem so pallid in comparison with the strength of the Arabic chant. Nevertheless, since the best can be the enemy of the good, it is important to state that access to sacred texts is not limited to those who know the original languages. An English loaf is better than none.

A holy text needs to be chewed thoroughly. The Greek fathers taught that in the Christian Eucharist, the bread was broken twice. First, the bread of the divine Word was broken by the interpretation of the sacred text; then the bread of the communion was broken in the Eucharistic meal. I find myself enthralled by the endless flow of commentaries on the most ancient of the classic religious texts. A Buddhist teacher of stature, Thich Nhat Hanh, a Vietnamese monk who was a friend of Thomas Merton, can throw new light on the ancient text we know in English as the Diamond Sutra. A rabbi stands up before a congregation in every synagogue on every Sabbath to uncover new meaning in the Torah portion, read yearly for some 2,500 years. The priest or minister breaks again each Sunday the bread of the gospels that have nourished so many for almost two millennia.

The fact that you are reading this essay may mean that reading is a yoga compatible with your path. If so, making the disciplined reading of a sacred text a part of your daily practice may make a great deal of sense. Thich Nhat Hanh gives sage advice at the beginning of his commentary on the Diamond Sutra when he tells us to read it with a serene mind, "a mind free from views." He encourages us to ask whether the words have anything to do with eating a meal, drinking tea, cutting wood, or carrying water. He seems to want us to approach the text from the viewpoint of what the poet Edna St. Vincent Millay calls "the mountain that you climb all day."

We have a New Testament study group at Lake Forest College. We meet once a week over lunch to "break the bread of the Word." I always point out to the students gathered there that this is not the place for some of the academic discussions that rightly characterize our classroom study of such texts. Here we gather to be nurtured by the Word, to find a name for that mountain we climb all day, to find teachings that speak to the meals we eat, the wood we cut, and the water we carry. The practice of *lectio divina*, in whatever sacred tradition, serves the purpose of leading us into the central mystery of that particular sacred path. This is how I would suggest you read any sacred text you choose for your *lectio divina*.

The Paradox of Practice

I remember a Common Ground program in which the religion journalist Roy Larson was the presenter. I forget the exact title of his talk, but I remember distinctly one of his new beatitudes: "Blessed are those who don't give a damn whether or not they're blessed." I was sitting next to a Buddhist friend of mine who immediately said to me: "Very Zen!"

There's an important truth in Larson's beatitude, and we need to keep it in mind. It is so easy to get caught up in the accouterments of our own practice. Zen Buddhists will even say of a too-fervent novice that he or she "stinks of Zen." "Novice fervor" was something older Jesuits laughed at as they watched the strained piety of the all-too-eager first-year men. I remember with some embarrassment my own novice experience when keeping my cassock free from wrinkles, or my genuflection flawless, pushed from my consciousness any weightier matters of religion.

When we consciously begin a path of practice, it is important to stay detached from the path. This whole topic is treated with marvelous insight in Chögyam Trungpa's book *Cutting Through Spiritual Materialism.* He certainly put his finger on something very important when he identified spiritual materialism as all our ego-centered sidetracks, appearing under the guise of spirituality and spiritual practice. Attachment to one's practice, judging the practice of others—these are powerful temptations lurking close to every spiritual path. Humility and a good sense of humor usually prove to be their best antidotes.

True humility is not of the Uriah Heep variety, modeled after the obsequious character created by Charles Dickens. Such "humility with a hook" is but another device of the always-hungry ego. The Chinese say that the ocean is the greatest body of water because it lies the lowest and is thus able to receive all the rivers and streams flowing into it. True humility is receptivity without ego distortion. And humor is a natural companion to humility—not the kind of humor that laughs at the expense of others, but a humor that appreciates the deep incongruity of oneself and all of one's ego paraphernalia. "Getting the point" along one's spiritual path is not unlike "getting a joke"; and moments of enlightenment have been known to appear in a burst of full-bellied laughter.

I find great wisdom in the Zen Buddhist teaching "Before I began the path, mountains were mountains and trees were trees; when I first embarked on the path, mountains were no longer mountains and trees were no longer trees; when I had spent some time on the path, mountains were mountains and trees were trees."

There is an awkwardness in beginning to walk a path, and reality is temporarily distorted. If you're first learning to hold a golf club, the proper grip will feel awkward; with practice, however, it will become natural. It's important to realize that in this Zen teaching, stage one and stage three are not the same. With practice, the ordinary is reachieved but at a higher level, where the duality between lack of enlightenment and enlightenment is being overcome. The culmination of all spiritual practice is "ordinary living."

It's what is profoundly natural. So too are the dance steps of Fred Astaire, but a great deal of practice preceded his naturalness and spontaneity on the dance floor.

There is a wonderful story in the Buddhist tradition about a disciple who asked his master to draw a cat for him. The master agreed, but then seemed to be putting him off for over a year. Finally, in a fit of frustration, the disciple asked for the picture. The master took a clean sheet of paper and, with just a few skilled motions, drew a marvelous cat. Instead of receiving the gift with gratitude, the disciple asked why it had taken the master so long to fulfill such a simple request, since he was obviously able to accomplish it in just a few seconds. With that, the master opened a closet behind him and hundreds of cat drawings tumbled to the floor. True mastery is effortless; but the way to mastery is by no means without effort.

EXPLORING A PATH

Symbol

My approach to reading a sacred text is based on the premise that the text has some kind of central structure, a central symbol on which it is hinged. I find it helpful to read the text outward from its central symbol.

I'm sure you've seen, whether in real life or in a movie, someone preparing to scale a wall by throwing up a grappling hook. The hook finally connects with some part of the parapet, and then the climb can begin. That's my favorite image of a symbol, since the etymology of the word *symbol* suggests something "thrown together." The symbol, in other words, originates in our mundane world of experience but serves as a grappling hook to link us to a transcendent reality. Working with various religious traditions, I have come to notice that each of these traditions (like their classic texts) has a central symbol.

Another metaphor for the function of a symbol is that of a window, in this case a window to the absolute. Like any window, it both allows those inside to see the larger world outside and allows the light from outside to enter the world inside. Or, you might say, the symbol functions like a two-way street, allowing the transcendent realm to reach the finite and giving the finite a way to the transcendent.

In Judaism, the central symbol is clearly the Torah, both in the narrower sense of the first five books of the Bible and in the broader sense of the teaching, Judaism's basic message. If we name this symbol from the divine side, then we celebrate the *matan torah*, the gift of the Torah, the understanding of the Torah as God's revelation to Israel. If we name this symbol from the human side, then it is the way the people of the Mosaic Covenant are called to walk the path that links them with the God of the Covenant. Reading the texts of Judaism from this central symbol outward can help us experience the coherence of the tradition. It thus allows for a more prayerful reading as well.

Unlike Judaism, Christianity finds its central symbol not in the sacred text but in a person, Jesus the Christ, God's Anointed One. When named from the side of transcendence, Christ is the Word of God, the Light of God, the Son of God entering our human sphere. But this same Christ can also be named from the side of our humanity, and then he is the Way to the Father, our model, our paradigm for a trusting response to God. Being aware of this twofold character of the central symbol helps us to organize the complex list of christological titles that we're faced with in the sacred texts constituting the Christian Testament. This in turn enables us to read the text more prayerfully since we're understanding the text in a direction from a core to a periphery, from a central symbol outward.

In Islam, as in Judaism, the central symbol is the text itself, in this case the holy Quran. Both Judaism and Islam clearly reject the centrality of the prophet who transmits the message from God. Neither Moses nor Muhammad are to be the objects of divine worship, nor should these two religions be named from their respective prophets. Judaism is not "the Mosaic religion," nor is Islam "Muhammadanism." The Christian Testament contains various genres of literature—gospels and letters primarily. But in the Quran we sense ourselves addressed directly by the divine Revealer. This makes sense when we realize that the writings of the Christian Testament are primarily telling us *about* the Christ but the Quran speaks to us directly from its divine source. Thus our prayerful reading of the Quran is from the Quran itself outward, from the divine Revealer to the community receiving the revelation.

When Thomas Merton, on his last pilgrimage, visited the immense statues of the Buddha at Polonnaruwa in Ceylon, he spoke of their great smiles, "filled with every possibility, questioning nothing, knowing everything." Surely Siddhartha Gautama, the historical Buddha, sitting in meditation, is the central symbol of Buddhism. All the Buddhist scriptures seem to resonate from that core image, sending out those same waves that Merton felt in the smiling statues. Our prayerful reading of the texts is enhanced when we read them from this direction, from this central symbol outward.

Myth

I've heard it said that Paul Tillich would sometimes pound his professorial podium and shout at his American class: "Never say '*only* a symbol'!" As we have seen, symbols are not deficient realities; they are quintessential realities. Symbols link us with the deepest mystery, the very Ground of Being. By the same token, in the language of comparative religious study, myths aren't mere fables but symbols in narrative form. This opens further for us the sacred texts we are engaging through our prayerful reading and the traditions they articulate. Not only can these texts and traditions be read from the central symbol outward, but we find that this symbol itself is expressed in a narrative form, a story. Again, it helps to look at this concretely.

I have said that the Torah is the central symbol of Judaism. Now as we look through the prism of the Torah, we grasp the central myth as well. It is, of course, the story we call "the exodus." The Jewish community chose this Greek title for the second book of the Torah when Jewish scholars translated the texts from Hebrew to Greek, around the second century B.C.E. in the thriving city of Alexandria. *Exodus* means "the way out." (If you drive around in Greece, every exit ramp is named "exodus," and that same word is stamped on your passport when you leave the country.)

Israel's central story is an exodus, a way out, a freeing up *from* the slavery of Egypt and a freeing up *for* a covenanted life with God. Both aspects of this experience are important since it would not make much sense to be freed up from slavery only to die in the desert of meaningless wanderings. Thus the first part of the story is the exciting narrative of escape. We think of Miriam, Moses' sister, leading the Hebrew women in the ancient verse "Sing to the Lord, for He has triumphed gloriously; horse and rider He has thrown into the sea." The other side of the story, of course, is when the people stand at Sinai and receive the Ten Commandments, thus entering into a convenanted relationship with God.

Christianity sees this drama replayed in the death and resurrection of Christ. The initiatory rite of Christian baptism is one in which the candidate goes down into the waters and emerges reborn. The transition is both from slavery to freedom—a crossing of the Sea of Reeds—and a participation in the death and resurrection of Christ. This narrative of the path from death to new life is the central myth or story of Christianity. It takes two basic forms among Christians today, as it did in the first-century world of the Jesus-believers as well. One type of Christianity, identified more with Paul, stresses the death of Jesus as the crucial factor in this transition from death to life. Another type of Christianity, linked in ancient times with the name of Thomas, understands this crucial movement as residing primarily in Jesus' teachings about taking up the cross and losing one's life to find it. In both cases, the movement from death to life characterizes the central myth.

The Quran urges us to recognize God in his signs. The very chanting of the Quran is such a sign. As we come to recognize God in his signs, our response is one of total submission. Submission, of course, is the actual meaning of the word *Islam*. A Muslim, quite simply stated, is one who submits to God. The myth then is the story of every human being who recognizes God in the signs of the created world and in the sign of the revealed Word of the Quran, and who then submits to this transcendent Revealing God, this one God, Allah, whose prophet is Muhammad. It is the prophet himself who most clearly exemplifies this recognition of signs and consequent submission. Nevertheless, the central myth is not his story alone but the timeless human story of recognition and submission. Islam understands itself not as a new religion but as a final restatement of the one religion given to humankind from the days of Adam.

In Buddhism, Siddhartha Gautama is but one of a myriad of buddhas. The story is not his alone but belongs to all of us. He made the transition from sleep to full wakefulness. The title "Buddha" means the one who woke up. We are all called to embody this quality of being awake. The silent and seated Buddha reminds us that the story takes place within our minds, in consciousness itself. For it is there that we realize the Four Noble Truths: that life has an unsatisfactory character (suffering); that our lack of satisfaction is rooted in illegitimate expectations (clinging); that this realization of the connection between clinging and suffering has within it the secret of the cessation of suffering (release); and finally, that release and enlightenment can be found in commitment to the Eightfold Path of right perspective, right resolve, right speech, right conduct, right livelihood, right effort, right mindfulness, and right concentration.

Ritual

If the symbol is our connecting link with the transcendent mystery, and if the myth is the symbol in narrative form, then what is ritual but the community enactment of the myth? The ritual may express the central myth itself or one of the many facets of that central myth as it radiates within the literature and the tradition. A good ritual should neither need nor tolerate extensive rational interpretation and commentary. Nothing is more frustrating in a ritual context than fumbling through a sheaf of papers to find the right page, and listening to endless explanations of what the community is doing. A good ritual should be self-evident; just experiencing it should communicate to you what's happening. Losing that clarity is a sure sign of ritual degeneration.

It is sometimes said that every great religion excels in something. If that is the case, then the Jewish claim is easily established. To paraphrase a popular Passover song, if Judaism had given us only the Sabbath, "it would have been enough—*dayyenu*." The Sabbath in its weekly rhythm celebrates the central myth of freedom. The environment of the home bespeaks the freedom of the participants in this ritual, for they do not eat standing like harried slaves but seated and at leisure. The opening gesture, the lighting of the Sabbath candles, reminds the participants that Israel was sanctified by the commandments that constitute its convenantal life and that the very lighting of the candles is the response to a *mitzvah*, a commandment. For the full twenty-four hours of the Sabbath, we breathe the air of freedom, the freedom to let God be God and to lay aside our human enterprises.

What the Sabbath celebrates each week is ritualized in greater detail once a year in the *seder*, the service that initiates the festival of Passover. I have worked for some twenty years now with the Jewish students here at Lake Forest College as they prepare the seder each spring. Every detail of the meal highlights one aspect of the story, the *Haggadah*. Unleavened bread reminds us of escaping slaves with no time for bread to rise, and bitter herbs put in our mouths the very taste of servitude. The same bread is eaten with a mixture representing the mortar used in the bricks the slaves were forced to make in Egypt. But freedom is celebrated too for we sit at leisure as only free people can. And we eat green herbs as a sign of springtime hope. The rabbis say that the Passover is rightly celebrated when those who have taken part in the ritual feel they have indeed left slavery and have stood at Sinai to receive the commandments leading to convenanted living.

The communion meal in Christianity parallels the weekly Sabbath celebration of Judaism, just as Easter parallels Passover. In an otherwise solar calendar, Easter and its allied celebrations depend on the moon. The feast is kept on the first Sunday after the first full moon that follows the vernal equinox. Pentecost is the seventh Sunday after Easter; Trinity Sunday is the Sunday after Pentecost; and Corpus Christi is the Thursday after Trinity Sunday. Thus all these feasts are movable ones, following the kind of patterns we see in the Jewish calendar, which is an adjusted lunar calendar so that holidays fall in the same season, though not on the same date. Islam has an unadjusted lunar calendar and thus holidays can occur at any time of the year.

This business of calendars may seem far afield, but I see them as closely allied to the central structure of symbol, myth, and ritual. Judaism's calendar begins with the year of creation as it is calculated from the biblical records of geneologies and life spans; Christianity begins its count of years with Jesus' birth; and Islam places as its starting year the time of Muhammad's flight from Mecca to Medina. Calendars, then, and the flow of liturgical feasts they contain, are valuable points of insight into the respective traditions they embody. A calendar is the way we keep the year together and also the continuity from one year to the next. The rituals flowing from a religious calendar contrast sharply with the secular seasons reflected in our department stores, where we move from pumpkins to turkeys to elves and bells, and then from hearts to colored eggs and bunnies, with a final flourish of fireworks in the summer.

In the communion meal, Christians remember their Lord in the breaking of the bread and the sharing of the cup. They are reminded of Jesus' life as God's servant, giving himself completely in love until his own body was broken and his very blood poured out. Thus they are reminded too that they are called to serve others, to love as Jesus loved, and to live as Jesus lived. This mystery, celebrated weekly in many Christian churches, is given heightened attention in the yearly celebration of Easter, the holiest of Christian holidays, the fullest expression of the movement from death to life, from crucifixion to resurrection.

I took one of my college classes to visit a nearby mosque. The imam was most gracious, and, as he spoke with us, he did something that impressed us deeply. He talked about Islam as meaning "submission" and then he said that the central expression of this is the ritual prostration used in the prayers that are said five times each day. We had just witnessed a time of prayer and were still standing on the carpeted floor of the mosque. The imam knelt down and stretched himself out in the traditional prostration. When he stood up, he said to us: "This is Islam." The action was so simple, so humble, and so revealing; it said more than any words he might have used. Such is the power of ritual. The prayers and prostrations constitute one of Islam's five pillars. It would be difficult to imagine a more fitting ritual for Islam's central myth and symbol.

The most essential Buddhist ritual is no more difficult to find. Buddhists of every variety—Japanese, Tibetan, Thai, Vietnamese, American—sit in meditation. It is a ritual that belongs to every spiritual path but to none more than Buddhism, whose founder woke up while seated under the Bo tree. The techniques of meditation differ, but in any of its varying forms it has certainly been Buddhism's greatest gift to the world of religion, what Buddhism does best. This is a practice all can share: Protestants, Catholics, Jews, Muslims, Buddhists, and those with no particular religious convictions or commitments. It is a truly universal home for the human spirit. Although I don't believe in any spiritual panacea, meditation is what I would recommend for almost anyone's first step on a spiritual path.

THE FRUIT

My parents took me to New York City when I was about twelve years old. We attended a solemn High Mass at St. Patrick's Cathedral with Cardinal Spellman presiding. I remember turning to my Protestant father and saying something about the impressive character of all that was transpiring. My father answered, "I don't recall Jesus saying a great deal about any of this pageantry, but he did say something about everything being known by its fruits." That telling comment serves as a good introduction to this final section of our exploration of spirituality. Much that goes by the name of spirituality today seems to be little more than another kind of narcissism. True spirituality is known by its fruits, and those fruits are wisdom and compassion.

I spoke of wisdom earlier, pointing out its unique characteristic of organizing knowledge in terms of a larger framework. So much of what constitutes modern life comes in isolated packages. Issues don't seem to touch. Experience is isolated and alienated. We hear so much about increased networks of communication, and yet many of us continue to fear that the speed of moving essentially trivial and transient information will not favorably affect the content. We are being buried in the detritus of our computer "bits" (an abbreviation of binary digits), but our thirst for spirit remains unslaked by this stream of digital signals.

Wisdom relates intimately to the pattern of symbol, myth, and ritual I described. Once we come to grasp the wholeness of a spiritual tradition in its texts and in its practices, understanding it outward from its central symbol and the narrative expression of that symbol, in the myth that is then concretized in ritual, we are on the path of wisdom. We have a way of living whole and integrated in the world. We have a basis for discernment, separating wheat from chaff, the transient from the permanent, the passing fad from the abiding current.

Wisdom blossoms naturally into compassion, as a tree bears fruit. This compassion is not a patronizing form of taking pity on someone. It is rather a true fellow-feeling for the other, stemming from a deep recognition that we are all one. Thomas Aquinas defined love as "willing the good of the other." True compassion wills nothing but the other's deepest good. Like Martin Buber's I-Thou experience, it "feels from the other side." In other words, we begin truly to experience reality from the viewpoint of the other, the one to whom we are speaking, the neighbor with whom we are relating in so many ways each day. And extending beyond our fellow human beings, the challenge of compassion directs our attention to all life and even to our planetary home that nurtures life so generously.

SUMMARY

Although there's no unanimity about the use of the two terms *religion* and *spirituality*, they are generally regarded as different aspects of one reality. In my own study of various religious traditions, I have noticed two premises that seem to underlie every form of religion. First, there is something of ultimate significance going on in the universe; and second, there is a way of being connected with it. The best guess for the etymology of the word *religion* has to do with some sense of this connectedness. This entire phenomenon then implies both the awareness of the ultimate mystery and the experience of participating in it.

It seems to me that the idea of religion points to this reality from its more observable, objective side. When you ask people about their religion, they generally point to a form of sociological identification. They say that they are Methodists or Buddhists,

Muslims or Hindus. But when you ask people about their spirituality, they respond in terms of the personal, subjective, and experiential side of this reality. They tend to talk about the way they
experience the world as a Methodist or Buddhist, the way they connect to reality as a Muslim or Hindu.

Religion tends to locate people within a group; spirituality
points to them as individuals. Three Zen Buddhists meditating in
the same zendo would still be different in their attempts to articulate their respective spiritualities. Our spirituality is in some ways as
individual as our fingerprint or our DNA code. It fits us like glove
to hand. Some people understand themselves as spiritual but without any reference to a religion. Other people seem to be clearly
religious and yet do not evince a sense of spirituality. Still others
combine both in the happy marriage most of us would hope to find.

Spirituality seems to connote a dynamism not necessarily present in a discussion of religion. Eastern traditions often speak about
this in terms of a movement towards enlightenment. One moves
from ignorance and sleepiness to wisdom and awareness. In the
Western religions we find more language about turning, repenting,
and being converted. One moves from ego-centered patterns of sin
to a more God-centered life of holiness. But in both cases, the
focus is on movement, however we describe that process of growth.
Like spokes of a wheel around a central hub, spiritual paths are
ways to the center. Speaking of spirituality emphasizes the experience of walking; speaking of religion emphasizes the nature and
identity of the path one walks.

At one level, the religion is the vehicle, and spirituality is the
movement achieved by means of that particular conveyance.
Buddhism speaks of itself as a raft; its purpose is to take us across
the river separating illusion from enlightenment. Clinging to the
raft after arriving at the farther shore makes no sense. Worshipping
the vehicle seems to be the besetting sin of most religions at one
time or another. But this form of in-house idolatry inevitably

proves more deleterious to authentic religion than any external enemy. Only the continuing emphasis on the process can check this imbalance. A happy marriage is possible only when religion and spirituality work together.

As I reread these pages, I sense so much that has not been said, but I hope this will suffice to give some sense of how we might begin to allow space for the spirit, both in our own personal lives and in our shared world. A spiritual friend or a support community is of great help. If such is not available, we have to rely on the wisdom we can find in sacred books. Prayerful reading of these texts, with a quiet receptivity to the mystery of holiness they contain, begins to give our spirits space. So too does the simple practice of meditation, a quiet centering of our souls. Life becomes simpler, more ordinary, and yet somehow more satisfying. Boredom begins to disappear because each moment tends more to open our eyes in wonder. There are fewer uninteresting or unworthy people since we see them increasingly as belonging intimately to us and to all that we are. An environment of dialogue begins to turn competitors into allies. Sorrow is there to feel, more poignantly than ever perhaps, but it is less perceived as "suffering." Compassion flows more freely from us, and yet it too is nothing special.

With the fourteenth-century mystic Dame Julian of Norwich, a deep faith grows in us that "all will be well, all will be well, every conceivable thing will be well."

WHERE PSYCHOLOGY ENDS

Lorette Zirker

PSYCHE AND SPIRIT

This essay appears in a book on spirituality. The book is meant to enliven the life of the spirit, if I may put it that way, so that the word "spirituality" is less slippery, less sentimental, more accessible to one's mental fingertips.

In thinking about this, I find I must first distinguish "psychology" from "spirituality," however they may weave and tangle with each other in one's life. I must do this because I have a gut feeling, underlying the definitions and images of each, that with thorough enlightenment comes a natural shucking off of the everyday psyche as we have known and loved it.

I want to be sure that I'm getting on with spiritual study as the all-embracing activity it is. I want to be sure I'm not confusing the solving of my own problems, and the relieving of my private anxieties, with the solving of larger, or different, mysteries. I have a strong feeling that the search for these solutions will place my personal worries in their proper context.

At this particular moment, I find it important to sort this out. The fact that I can see that this *is* a confusion is interesting.

One of the signals that alerted me to work on this again was some reading in current American Zen teaching and practice. I was suddenly alarmed by a few books and manuscripts—only a few, true—that seemed to be stressing techniques of handling one's own problems instead of stressing the disciplined search for spiritual understanding *out of which* one might then have some success in handling one's own problems.

I'd hesitate to say that this is a typically American pothole for Zen students because I have no direct experience with what the rest of the Western world is doing with the Zen Buddhist spirit. But it's certainly our tendency to be very practical with whatever we're learning and to see new knowledge, whether logically or mystically gained, in terms of possible applications.

Another signal came one day out of memory, a memory of my pre-Zen past, when my spiritual interest was just an eddying breeze, but everyone and his brother were being told to "see a psychiatrist." This was before the great growth of pharmaceutical psychiatry and during the heyday of "adjustment." Other people were referred to as well adjusted, or maladjusted, by those who may or may not have had direct experience of psychiatric analysis. The terminology used to scare me to death. The trouble was that gut feeling again. I *knew* there was more to life than merely society, but I didn't know the word *spirituality*, and I was, of course, by social conditioning, "against religion."

It's fair to ask me why, when Buddhist spirituality begins with the Buddha's understanding of "suffering" and the ways to alleviate and reduce it, I should fuss about an overemphasis on the psyche.

The answer is that when we spend a lot of time watching ourselves grasping and clinging—two causes of suffering—we tend to forget, or never to learn, *why* grasping and clinging are so useless.

My view is that we're doing all this spiritual study and practice for the sake of the larger Spirit; we're not using the Spirit in order to "become whole" or whatever the phrase is. We may in fact be "integrating" along the way, but we're doing it for Spirit's sake, or within its activity. This is the reverse of what I've been reading lately.

I'll try to make clearer what I'm calling psychology and what I'm calling spirituality for the purpose of this piece. I'll refer to three themes, or conditions: detachment, dwelling in limbo, and manifestation. Somewhere along this way, it will become clearer, to both of us, why my impulse is to pursue the spiritual explorations as deeply as possible and not accept mere personal ease as the goal.

I'd settle for a little personal ease. Often.

But I see it now as an intermediate comfort, something relieving and encouraging. The posture I really want to be in is the one that sees personal ease as a condition and personal hurt and confusion as conditions. The posture I want is the one that has entered fully into all these conditions, but also is ready for "Yes, yes, I see what that comes out of."

This is what here I'm calling psychology: concern for myself. Concern for my mental state, for my physical condition, in general and at any moment; for my relationships with other human beings; and for my economic and political self and societal position. (These are a few of my psychology things.)

In other words, I'm defining it as affairs of the personal, relative plane rather than of the Absolute; affairs of phenomena; matters of temporal agitation rather than of abiding equanimity. I think these are matters of samsara, the daily round, the world in which we see ourselves living, the world of wars and weddings, of deaths inexplicable to the survivors, and of friendships that bloom in alien soils. And of all the random life that we try to organize and rationalize, all the bruises, the urgent motivating, the apparent struggles and the apparent triumphs.

This is what we bring with us to the cushion, the kneeler, and the prayer mat because we are, after all, "human."

Now this is what I'm calling spirituality: the knowing (and you *know* you know) that there must be another way of looking at things that is ultimately less perilous and more sensible and unburdening.

If I could only maintain this other way of looking at things, I wouldn't worry so much. I'd be more relaxed, forgiving, and compassionate. I'd have a little space to look around and see a bit more clearly why the world is in the mess it's in (what state is it really in?) and perhaps what I might do about that.

This other way of looking at things—this shift in perspective—gives me a much clearer look at my own affairs in the larger picture. The much larger picture. It offers some ways around and through my personal, self-absorbing jungle. There's a lot more knowledge—dare I call it wisdom?—available to me, for temporal solutions, than I ever thought possible. And there's a bit of safety, a net, a rock here and there to hold me while I work things through with much more clarity and confidence.

But it's my contention that if spirituality is presented only in the light of psychology, in terms, that is, of problem-solving and obstacle-dissolving, it will get lost in tool-using vocabularies. It will be presented as useful; and the users will never continue to explore it for its own sake, on its behalf, for their universal lives.

Secondarily, the users will find their problems reappearing, in new entanglements, and will become more and more disheartened.

In my experience, the experience of age and some practice, the wiser course is to bumble through the immediate aches with much humility and a lot of "I don't understand's," putting aside the hurts and frustrations for later examination (will they still be there?), and instead, vigorously going for the evolving spiritual realization. Along the way, a great many amazing things happen. I think teachers must present this amazement with enthusiasm.

A tool for the undergraduate contemplative, which takes one right out of a tool-using vocabulary, is detachment. Here is one aspect of it.

A few weeks ago I saw an old movie for the third or fourth time: *Captain Newman, M.D.*, with Gregory Peck. But on this viewing, something happened. I became aware, at a new level, that it was possible to look at a painful or insoluble or paralyzing problem with an inquiring mind. My attitude to what's difficult is, all too frequently, a fatalistic abandon. Run! Some people bring a zealous idealism to difficulties, but I've always recoiled from the zeal. So, all negative.

I thank the art of Gregory Peck for giving life to Captain Newman's ability to view his wartorn patients with sincere inquiry. It wasn't until this viewing of the movie that I could see my habitual withdrawal and defeat in the face of difficulty. It was the opposite of an inquiring mind seeking clear comprehension. There was revealed an entirely different point of view I could apply to pain and mystery of whatever depth.

Take the matter of a recalcitrant sewing machine. Take the matter of Bosnia. Take the matter of my neighbors who love Oliver North. Take China and Tibet. Take a smiling, smug, poisonous male chair of the public library board. Take a new computer program. Take gang fights in Albuquerque, of all places. Take the children of old friends who yell at their parents with blame. Take a vacuum cleaner that puts down instead of picking up.

Run! Flee! Hide! Explode!

My Zen training included trying to notice how I handle the circumstances before me. I noticed, but I transform very slowly. However, I learned to observe more.

I observe a friend sit down at my sewing machine, saying, "What does it do?" The correct answer to this question is not "It wrecks the whole neckline! Sewing machines always do this to me!"

The correct answer has something to do with thread and stitch size and tension, all witnesses to the inquiring mind. I observe my friend fix the machine, fix the neckline, and fix me with the shriveling comment, "I love to figure out what's wrong."

Now, is this spiritual?

Yes, I'm afraid it is.

Afraid, because I didn't find it lofty, and it's damned hard work.

But the fact is, it is this attitude of my friend, this observing and this inkling of a thought of a possibility that there's another way to look at things that is the beginning of a more embracing, and ultimately melding, life. Embrace the sewing machine with care and attention, demonstrated my friend, and embracing the universe and being embraced may come later. If that's what you think you want. At this time.

Yes, naturally, I didn't see it then.

And yes, as far as action goes, handling the problem by taking the machine—gently—to the repair shop and describing—calmly—the jammed needle would have been more meritorious, as the old traditions use the word, than trying rebelliously to fix it myself.

There are choices of behavior. However, I now think that spiritually, there's no choice but to look at what's in front of you, with whatever bit of spirit—or "gumption," as Pirsig says—you can muster. With, strangely enough, an inquiring mind.

This connection, or Very Fine Line, between matters of the spirit and matters that seem to be behavioral is tricky. It's taken me almost thirty years of practice to see it. A clue may lie in the word *fear*, which we tend in our culture to define psychologically, thereby limiting our understanding of it. There's more dimension to fear, I've just been finding out, than the psychological. Eido Roshi says, "Confront bravely!" but that's not simple. English-speaking people who adopt the word *angst* instead of *anxiety* have had hints that there's more to anxiety than the psychological dimension.

Meanwhile, we've left Gregory Peck with his wartime psycho-logical casualties. What I understood on this viewing of *Captain Newman* was that the psychiatrist's mind was not as frozen as mine, as these problems continued through more wars. The good doctor, with a little confidence, a little love, and some knowledge and train-ing, was actually inquiring into the awkward behaviors of his patients. He liked to figure out what was wrong. He was afraid only of his momentary inadequacy in a given circumstance. He asked the right questions. He looked at his patients clearly. He was engaged, I suddenly saw, in spiritual practice.

God knows why I needed this highly specialized situation, fic-tionalized and dramatized at that, to pull together a large number of spiritual threads. Maybe it was because of what Eido Roshi calls "the readiness of time" for me. Maybe it was because I suddenly saw an expression on the actor's face I had missed previously: the moment when he himself realized what Captain Newman had to understand about his work.

Detachment is a tricky word in English. (I'm always mindful of the translators in this migration of Eastern tradition to the West.) "Coldly detached" is a frequent usage and a negative one. It seems to mean absenting yourself from the living situation in front of you. Disdain is in the air. Sometimes, contempt for the processes of inquiry.

Disinterest is a similar word to which we add a coolness. You don't hear about someone diving disinterestedly into a situation.

I want to drop the literary usage of the word *detachment* and use it as a Buddhist technical term. I now see detachment plainly, unemotionally, as a spiritual act.

What should I be detaching from, in order to clear my inquir-ing mind? The answer is: the extras. The presupposition, the habit, the bias, the history. And vanity, fear, and other voices. See those extras (ah yes, somewhere along the line I should be learning to see them) and let them all go, for a moment or two at least. The inquiring mind doesn't need them. As Pirsig quotes from his translated motorcycle manual: First, have peace of mind.

Detaching is breaking out of the jungle growth, even momentarily. Just long enough to see, perhaps, that an assessment of mechanical repair doesn't require strangling ourselves with vines of emotion; that individuals are in the middle of their own problems and can barely see us through their own undergrowth, much less threaten us.

One evening in Hawaii, at a dinner party with good food and no other content, I was standing on the balcony watching the ocean. It was sunset and the light was catching the foam on the wave-curls. The bay was wide and shallow, and the rollers were long and slow. And all of a sudden, they were rolling in all by themselves.

Well, yeah. Of course.

No. Up to then, apparently, I had been willing them in.

You may laugh, but I must have had something to do with it because suddenly I didn't. They were on their own. I was watching them do it on their own.

"Without your pushing them, the clouds roll by. (If they can do without you, ducky, so can I.)"

It lasted a fraction of a second. What a wonder! I was then a very new Zen student, but I knew this was important. Days later I tried to explain it, but I didn't get to quite the right person.

"The waves came in by themselves!"

"Yeah? So see you Wednesday night."

I turned to my Catholic-trained friend, and in her tobacco-smoked kitchen I said, "But I have to swallow first, or blink my eyes or something to see them again, and that doesn't always work, but I know it's important."

"Well," she rasped, "keep at it."

Begin; then go on. Advice from ancient Zen master.

But there seemed to be no context to put this into, to support it.

It didn't seem to be part of mu practice, but then I didn't know what that was all about anyway. So every few months or years I'd try to do this trick of flipping over, of letting the waves roll in, and sometimes the trick worked for a fraction of a second, and mostly it didn't.

And so it went for about fifteen years of reading and trying to raise a family and idiosyncratically practicing Zen.

Then one day I was in charge of a leaf-raking crew of four at a monastery. One member understood more than I did about the importance of this ditch we were clearing, and other things, and she went about her business. One member simply sat down on a rock and said, "I'm so tired." And one weekend visitor said to me, all eager, "What should I do?" I heard myself say, "Watch the leaves being raked."

She stared at me for a moment, then nodded cheerfully, saying softly as she got to work, "Okay, watch the leaves being raked. Watch . . ."

"Watch, and pray." That's a quote from Zooey or Buddy via J. D. Salinger, via the Bible I think.

Paying attention. With awareness. Mindfully.

Here it was; the switch. The switch that was mental (mental?) to back up the physiological blinks and gulps. The switch that combined all those Buddhist admonitions and strained efforts.

("Pay attention!"

"I *am* paying attention. Jeez.")

Well, I'm a slow learner.

I wanted to fall down on the stony road and do a full prostration, something that had never appealed to me before.

For years after, even though I tried to remember, I would flick that switch only when reminded by something I was reading, or once in a great while as I did the dishes. I still didn't really know where "mindfulness" came into spirituality. Appreciation, maybe? Concern? A couple of precepts?

Doing the dishes, by the way—a slight digression here, but

everything connects, trust me—can be a highly esoteric practice. Apart from the very occasional recollection of the switch, something else happens that's quite involuntary: I'll remember a fragment of a dream.

Now, if you've got your right brain and left brain hypotheses straight you'll know that, very roughly, the left brain is the more analytical and the right brain is the more intuitive.

We did some art exercises once at the monastery, led by a senior member and artist, out of the book about drawing with the right side of the brain. Ego, in the matter of drawing skills, certainly showed up during that meeting. But more important, I overheard the most senior member say quietly to Roshi: "The right brain is what we're trying to get at, isn't it?"

The exercises were very hard for me and took great concentration. And time after time, my forgotten dreams of the night before popped up, for milliseconds, but enough to recognize a scene or feeling. At one point I said aloud, "This must be working" (whatever I meant by working) "because I keep tapping into my dreams." Nobody reacted to that, but I've become fairly grown up about nonreactions, with practice. However, I realized that Most Senior Member had said something very important, and I had experienced a glimpse of it, and I would remember it. Did this also have something to do with koans?

Dishwashing, for me at least, opens a hatch sometimes. I can't knowledgeably take this any further. Suffice it to say, the most mundane activities can produce the most startling spiritual products if—if what?

If we pay attention?

And pay it not to the startling possibilities, but to the dish!

Back to the switch, or flip.

Could I be switching off the left brain in that moment? Am I closing the analytical circuits, just briefly, and leaving pure action? Is that what detachment really is? Are paying attention and detachment the same thing? Is all this, mindfulness? Is this the manner in which mindfulness is spiritual?

But then, who is raking the leaves?

"*'Ah,' said Lady Yü.*"

The trouble with the switch was that it didn't stay clicked. It eased off unnoticed, within seconds. Then it took a complicated set of patterns of memory and physiology to click it on again, weeks or months later.

It didn't become a habit. And it wasn't understood at a deeper level than "good habit."

I think this was because it was still my secret. My own little practice. My own imagery; my own experiences dealing with it. I knew even more clearly that it was important, at least to me, but it didn't have the sanction of tradition or the support of modern expertise.

But wait a minute: Who is it that's raking the leaves?

That formulation has a very Zen ring to it. One of the ancients asked, "Who is it that is doing zazen?" Who is it that is cooking the rice? Who is it that is asking?

("*Who that up there?*"

"*Who that down there?*"

"*Who that up there sayin' 'Who that down there?'?*")

Who is it, or what is it, that's doing the dishes if I'm not?

If the question had been translated What is it? wouldn't that have pushed a student along a little more directly? Maybe not. I, for one, would have said: Oh yeah, the Tao, the Dharma, God, etc., but after all, I'm the Who. Who else is there?

Let me take a sideways path here but it does circle back, with a bushel of leaves. I want to bring in the idea of confidence.

How does one gain confidence? I mean, confidence in something connected with risk.

Repetition helps. If you do something a certain number of times, it gets easier; never mind for the moment the question of where your original spurt of courage came from. And if something intriguing happens a certain number of times, you begin to gain a little confidence that it might happen again. Further, you begin to get a whiff of connection.

Zen doesn't say much about coincidence. But coincidences are fun. And I've noticed that people who remark on many coincidences in their lives also wax lyrical-spiritual about it. "Somebody out there is watching over me, ha-ha." "There are things seen and unseen." "There are more things in heaven and earth, Horatio . . ."

Enough whiffs of connection, whether you think of them as coincidence, or luck, or pattern—for instance, people appearing in your life, then totally disappearing, as if their task were done—and you have to begin to wonder.

These are very small jigsaw pieces to a very large operation, as it were. People experience a larger whole, or Higher Mind, or The Something, in different ways, in or out of crisis circumstances. My point here is that I couldn't be told anything about the flukey idea of connection. I couldn't be urged to believe it on the basis of authority or history. I had to have my own experience and the open eyes to see the experience for what it was. But I "prayed" for courage, and courage arose to meet need. When I couldn't make a decision, the decision decided itself. I wanted to go one way; that way was often blocked.

After a while, if you notice these things, the apparent setbacks and the galling frustrations, as well as the respondings and the smoothings, you begin to gain a little confidence in the workings of that thing out there that you don't "control." Confidence, first, that maybe it exists. Confidence, second, that maybe it knows more than you do. Confidence, third, that it keeps functioning whatever you do or think or want for yourself or believe about it.

And confidence, eventually, that it is the Who or What. Or at least you are partners, maybe. Or anyway you yourself have *something* to do with all this, right? But it's still a bit of a mystery exactly how. In the meantime, you'll just watch it operating and try to observe how you fit in and, even, to what extent you might rely on it if you absolutely had to.

Home with the leaves and the leaf-rake.

This is detachment: observing it happen. Having the confidence that it *will* happen. Somehow you're effecting something, even though you're not straining and striving, or dictating and manipulating. It's happening without your criticisms, your judgments, your needs for measurement and reward, your objections and obstinacy; even without your operatic displays of energy. Two phrases come out of the ether: "Be still, and know that I am God." And the Buddhist "Do nothing."

We finished the raking job, for that year. Where did the energy come from? The sit-down member eventually got up and started raking. What, really, is peer pressure?

In short, all the vanities that are Me are really unnecessary to raking leaves and washing dishes. The accomplishment of these feats doesn't even take any kind of piety or devotion.

Well, this is quite a detachment.

But don't I count for anything?

All I can tell you, after wrestling with this for a long time, is that this question changes. It is absorbed into the wider mystery of how it all works.

Believe it or not, ability and energy grow. Effectiveness grows. Above all, creativity as motive power grows, volt by volt. And you suddenly find yourself saying: What was the question?

Thus, the self-absorbed mind becomes the inquiring mind. And this problem-solving, detoxifying mind needs only to watch, to observe, detachedly. With this detached mindfulness, one begins to gain confidence in the larger workings of the Something and in its amazing energy.

I have an inkling, a glimmer, that at some point complete trust, or Ultimate Confidence, overwhelms the need for remembering the switch, and one will live fundamentally in the On mode, out of psychology and into spirituality, which will of course no longer need to be called spirituality.

The following may seem like a long jump from watching the leaves being raked but it's a natural, progressive jump.

You remember that koanical question: Where do you go from the top of the hundred-foot pole?

I don't know the canonical answer to that, but lately I've been using the picture of that situation—there I am, having stepped off the top of the pole—to illustrate an invented phrase: Definite Limbo.

It's limbo first; the support of "definite" comes later, along with that confidence I mentioned. That's why this is a progressive jump. Or leap. (I'm using "limbo" in its everyday sense, not its formal, theological usage as the border between heaven and hell. That's a different set of images.)

Many people experience this disorientation of limbo after a shock. If you can recall the feeling after you've bumped into something, or suddenly tripped, or more seriously lost something important, like your car keys, or the use of your writing hand, or your job, or someone close to you, that's an experience of limbo. Momentum, or gravity, is missing or is your enemy. Whole chunks of life as you've lived it have vanished. There are big gulfs of nothingness. In the case of a death, the feeling lasts almost long enough for us to learn something, if we only knew what that was.

Throwing the switch, or detaching, revealed this gulf. I wouldn't have called it limbo at the time. But there was that feeling of If I'm not doing it, who is? Who is raking? And if *I'm* not needed, am *I* really standing here? Where should I stand? With shocks and losses, where *can* I stand solidly, reliably? Nothing's stable. Nothing's permanent.

Impermanence. Aha! You see how these Buddhists always have a word for it.

But where do you hang out, in impermanence?

"Simple," they tell you, with a wave of a wrinkled, spotted hand. "Dwell!"

To me, *dwelling* is a rather cozy, gravity-centered word. (Again, be aware of translations.) Therefore to dwell, hanging in midair over a gulf or chasm, is difficult to imagine. Dwelling in limbo is no easier to imagine. But the experience itself is a bit more concrete. We've all hung in limbo a few times in our lives. It *is* a defined situation we know we'll be in again. It's a definite limbo.

Whether I throw the switch myself while doing something safe like stirring the spaghetti, or whether something else throws it for me—skidding the car off the icy road and turning it around to face uphill—the limbo, I'm arguing, is the same. It requires the same spiritual confidence to recover the leaped-out heart. Moreover, the old stories tell us that this, this momentary absence of control as we've known it, is Reality.

Now here's one of the many bits I have to work out and it's probably only a matter of language again, but I'm stuck with language for the time being. Dwelling in impermanence, or continuing to function while merely watching things function, takes a lot of guts, not to mention some extra flippers or gills or semicircular canals. Where am I going to get that kind of equipment and that kind of courage?

I think the answer is, I will increase my skill and confidence by repeated experience and draw the trust from a number of sources but primarily from the Source.

(Indeed, eventually I will relinquish myself to the Source altogether, whereupon it will no longer be a Source.)

The words *dwell-trust* seem to go together much better than *dwell-impermanence* or *dwell-detachment*. One reason that the teachings of Buddhism appear to be so difficult to integrate into one's life and personality is that the words often seem incompatible or contradictory. Maybe that's because they're leading beyond one's life and personality. What's most annoying is the peekaboo hint that words, while essential, are not really essential.

Never mind. I'm still moving with gluey feet in samsara and I need words.

Trust.

This is hard to do in an "exotic" religion, not to mention an esoteric religion. It's hard to do in any religion, for most Americans. One of the reasons many of us looked into Buddhism was precisely because it said Don't take anything on trust; find out for yourself. But to what extent is this possible?

> "He took away the person, took away the environment, molding and fashioning first-rate disciples."
> —Burton Watson's translation
> from the preface to *The Lin-Chi Record*

> "Snatching away the man, or the surroundings, he shaped and fashioned superlative students."
> —Ruth Sasaki's translation of the same

> ". . . mind and body, fallen away . . ."
> —common translation from Master Dogen

These quotes are difficult. You say to yourself: If they take everything away, what's left? If I'm wiped out altogether, what's the point? A first-rate dead disciple?

Furthermore, it's hard to picture someone else doing this to you, except in terms of humiliation or brainwashing or some socially or politically obnoxious practice, in a fearful setting where the other has total command. (Hence the ambivalence about Zen practice in earlier years when the word "ego" was often misused.)

But I think these quotes describe the deeper results of throwing the switch or having the switch thrown. To see it this way, you have to be able to move back and forth from thrower to throwee, so to speak. Either way, you get the same effect. You end up with a person who has shucked off, or is shucked of, a lot of personal garbage, including a personal, unworkable concept of "control."

Normally we have no experience of how to function when there's nothing to function with and no circumstance or environment that might need us to function in.

Now as I understand this uncomprehending state of mind, it exists because we're normally stuck in one dimension, in one kind of thinking, at one viewing point. Some names for this dimension or usual level of operating are: relative; temporal; phenomenological; samsaric; existential (meaning "existing," as Eido Roshi uses it, not as Sartre uses it); and also—I think I'm right in this context—*Olam Hazeh*, "in the world of history." This dimension is what I'm calling, in this piece, psychology.

But a little observation—little, because the interval of light may be a second here and there but occurring over decades—shows that when you are switched over into that watch-it-being-done state, your own body and your own mind can be said to have fallen off. If a teacher can somehow contrive by "skillful means," by helping throw the switch, to give you a glimpse of pure functioning, pure activity, without the burdened person, and outside of comfortable, familiar circumstances, then at that moment she is looking at the makings of a good student: a student with a mite of direct experience that gradually can be expanded into a trusting confidence in another viewing point. That other dimension might be named absolute; eternal; essential; fundamental; nirvanic; or *Olam Haba*, "the world of eternity or infinity."

In other words, the student will begin to dwell, as Huang Po says, "firmly unattached," or in secure and Definite Limbo. It is a place from which the deeper dimensions will begin to reveal themselves. This is a dwelling place from which unencumbered activity and unobstructed functioning can arise, *as the Absolute may require it*. It's in the nature of an introduction to, a first taste of, what I'm calling here spirituality.

But is that activity then going to be colorless, boring, automated, lacking pizzazz? What happens to personality, flair, idiosyncrasy, distinctive flavor?

Ah.

MANIFESTATION

I've just endured a recurring mortification that comes with ordering clothes by phone. (It also comes in dressing rooms with three-sided mirrors, but I rarely do that anymore.) That is, I have to say out loud, and have it recorded, that I want to order the top in one size and the bottom in a larger size. Nobody at that moment cares that spirit is absolutely formless.

Maura O'Halloran wrote a little poem (in *Pure Heart, Enlightened Mind*) that says,

> *I was not born*
> *I will not die*
> *for I am*
> *nothing.*
> *But please do not*
> *stand on my*
> *toe.*

This is a marvelous statement of the Absolute and the Relative.

However, the word *nothing*, like the word *emptiness*, bothers me. Surely the English language can come up with something a little more instructive. When I'm standing there with the phone in one hand and the damning tape measure in the other, it's a little difficult to believe, with Maura-san, that "I am nothing."

Happily, I've found a couple of other words that suit my present degree of understanding a little better. Maybe I'll graduate to the big, total words someday. So far, *nothing* conveys nothing. The translators have done me wrong. Meanwhile, my interim words are *Source* and, for the mail-order me, *manifestation. Source* has a number of variations, including the Something; Potential; Tao; Spirit Mother (or Father) or Great Spirit; or anything else you want to use that implies eternal possibility plus a kind of inevitability. As I've said, these are probably undergraduate concepts, but at least they're instructive until I reach the end of all concept.

Manifestation has a nice detached feeling about it. That is, detached from me-me-me. I'm a manifestation of something else. I'm manifesting something else. There is manifesting. It's happening in two different sizes, this year.

So where does pizzazz come in?

Let's go back a little bit.

You may have noticed a certain breath-holding quality to Definite Limbo. Yes, it's secure in the sense of eternal, steady, continuing. But it has a suspenseful quality as well. Because it's "firmly detached," it sees all and embraces all. There's a cool feeling of possibility about it. Yes, we dwell in it, but when we go forth into the world of activity, the world of birth and death, we carry with us some of the possibility. In limbo, we've been holding our breath with shock and surprise; and then perhaps catching our breath. Then, having been "inspired," maybe without realizing it, we can begin activity on the out-breath, using all the possibility that was given to us.

This is only one metaphor out of many that try to describe the relationship between the Source and the manifestation; the Absolute and the Relative. (I hesitate to use "Creator and creature" here because of differences in East-West thinking.)

An often-used Eastern image is that of the ocean and the wave. Out of the mothering ocean is formed the wave of that moment, that combination of circumstances, in that particular place, its form and characteristics completely different from those of any other wave. A unique manifestation, yet certainly a part of the ocean.

So my picture is that we come forth into activity with a singular set of tools and propensities (and allergies). We exhibit ourselves in the temporal world as a particular body with certain tendencies and with a fairly clear mind that, unfortunately, becomes gradually more cloudy and burdened.

I can see now that watching the dishes being washed has two advantages, or, to put it another way, there are two services being performed. One is detachment from the activity. The second is modification of the activity.

We've talked a little about detachment. Let's see what modification means.

Nobody washes dishes the way this manifestation does. I realized this acutely at a potluck party when two dear friends, a not-yet-married couple, bickered over the best way to handle the flood of utensils and serving dishes pouring into the community kitchen. They happen to be two of the most judgmental people I know, and clearly there was a right and a wrong way in each mind. Faint effusions, almost of contempt, arose from the sink area. Everybody else backed out of the way.

I would have done things quite differently myself; so, I suppose, would each of the other guests. I remember how we were taught in junior high home economics, with the half bar of kitchen soap in its long-handled sudsing basket. I remember my mother's routine—quite different. I worked up my own. With a family it changed again. And how different now, washing up for one or two. Is it any wonder that friends shoo you away from their sinks? What could be more unique than doing the dishes? Dear readers, never fear for your individuality.

Now, what happens when I go into the let-it-be mode? Do I now begin to conform to some archetype of Dishwashing? Nonsense. What happens is that I suddenly wake up and see that I forgot to put any detergent at all in the dishpan and that I'd better soak that label off the syrup bottle because my half-conscious scraping at it hasn't accomplished a thing. I'm modifying my activity (in a large sense, bringing it into harmony) based on clearer observation. Does that sound terribly remote and "sacred" and ritualized? On the contrary, it was remote when I was unmindful. With the observing eye, it becomes efficient and productive if still not terribly interesting. But then I've forgotten about interesting or boring or any other personal adjective for the moment because I'm just too busy observing. This forgetting, or nonarising, is also saving me the wear and tear of getting annoyed, fatigued, or overstimulated from thinking about something else. It also saves bickering in public places among friends who otherwise love you. And the final product is, demonstrably, a set of clean dishes, the object after all.

What I've noticed, as experience follows experience, is that the more I throw the switch, the more a distinctive me shows up. This was a surprise. It's the opposite of what I expected at the beginning.

I thought that if I gave up control, even in this private, invisible way, I would be giving up my own self. I would be saying "Take me. Here's my intellect; who needs it? Here's my aesthetic sense; who agreed with it anyway? Here's my singularity; a nuisance in this chaotic world."

But wait. What does actually happen? Just a couple of examples (reconstructed after the events):

- While listening impersonally to two people with an increasingly egotistical scheduling problem, I saw a neat way to solve it.

- While lending a reluctant ear to the tale of someone's anxiety-ridden short-term money problem, I thought of a way to bridge the gap.

- Faced with an utterly intractable wardrobe problem of my own, my only solution obviously was to stay home in bed, whereupon a perfectly wearable combination occurred to me, accessories and all.

Instead of becoming a cipher without a mind of its own, I saw a mind clicking away, raising and discarding possibilities and lighting on good solutions. It used its own mysterious circuits and its own materials and metaphors. But it was working without the restrictions and constrictions generated by a persona with a history and an attitude. In more demanding moments than those above, it showed an intelligence that had hardly ever been exercised and a creativity that had never really flowered. Was it my own? Who else was being hugged, with thanks?

These, you may say, are not "serious" problems. No, but they are confidence-building stepping-stones to Trust. They point towards the day when heavier assaults on the self can be met with equanimity, as they were not in earlier life. Again I see why they call it Practice.

Please remember that I'm not talking here about psychology. I'm not using spiritual study to wash the dishes better. Please be clear. These examples show the *effects* of deeper spiritual under-standing and practice, not the goals. Of course behavior will be affected, modified, sooner or later, by a growing understanding and maturity in the work. Samsara is nirvana. "Form is emptiness; emptiness, form." How else does "the mysterious truth of Tathagata" reveal itself? How else is God known but by manifesta-tion? A Source, for what?

Greater efficiency and productivity are not the reasons for Dwelling, for renewing and recollecting by Detaching. The reasons are nonrational; are right-brained; are outside, for the moment, the intellect's and the psyche's domains. In Western terms, using Ron Miller's words, they are to practice our "vocation as human beings." It is to do "what we were called into being for—continuing God's sustaining of the world." In Eastern terms, we study and practice to "realize" the waves and the ocean and to "actualize" that existence-essence we have "awakened" to.

This is the place, I think, to bring in a variation of the thrown switch. I call it the blank wall. This is where I deal with the word *Creativity*, which is not one of my favorites.

Staring into a blank wall appears to be the opposite of watching things happen, but it's just another form of giving over control.

Why does giving over control belong in a chapter about mani-festing anyway?

Here's why.

The blank wall is what I look at in my mind when I'm trying to think of exactly the right word. I know just what I need to fit into the particular circumstance I'm describing or explaining but I can't think of the perfect word. This is a small bit of Pirsig's "stuckness."

What I'm really doing is looking for inspiration. I do that by dwelling in limbo for as long as it takes and then suddenly I see the word or the solution. Some people say they hear it. Looking at this process another way, it seems to me I did all I could and then I handed my stuckness over. The reason we don't always see this hand-over is that it's usually a matter of seconds or less, and we don't usually sanctify it with a prayer for help. There isn't time, and we're too busy concentrating, and the problem is so mundane. "Not just 'blue'; what's that color her eyes are?" "What can I do with these five leftover noodles?" (Even the solution of using the the-saurus, or a cookbook, is inspired.)

But out of nowhere comes the answer.

And don't ever inquire too minutely into how you solve cross-word puzzles, or astrophysical problems. You will rationalize your-self into paralysis. You couldn't have worked them out on a computer no matter how complex your software. Why?

It's because only I am I. Nobody else sees noodles as building blocks the way I do. Nobody else knows what I'm trying to get across to my reader through the medium of eye color. Nobody else remembers an anecdote Professor G told you about her childhood as the two of you walked across campus that day, which you now link with an image from her lecture, which ties in with what Colleague A was saying last year about. . . . Only you have access to all this information and intent and bias, and the emotional plasma that oozes in, no matter what.

Where is all this stored—the stuff you know, or once knew, or didn't know you knew?

In my imagery, it's all stored in the Source. And it's available in the form only you need, only to you. It's all there, every bit of it. Where else could it be? But it takes a manifestation to use it. It's my "creativity" that puts together the bits and pieces. It's my personality that draws them from the storehouse, that uses them to continue to shape that personality and manifest it in the working world.

There lies the pizzazz.

But I try very hard to bear in mind that this creative, productive process all started with handing over control for a moment, letting something happen, watching for an answer, being carried into the making of a wave.

Two little notes here.

One, I'm not sure I could carry on a discussion of free will with an earnest Western philosopher, seeing absolute, relative, and manifestation the way I do at this moment. Not in her terms, anyway.

Two, I'm pretty sure that the traditional quote attributed to the Buddha, "I alone am the World-Honored One," cannot be understood in the language of Western philosophy. I'm also pretty sure that Jesus' statement "I am the Way . . ." has been largely misunderstood by his noncontemplative Western adherents.

Finally: For the image of manifestation, emerging directly, clear-eyed and uncluttered from formlessness, I often remember a wonderful scene from *M.A.S.H.*

A very large, impressive, and exotic-looking man is standing in the camp.

Hawkeye says, "Do you have any identification?"

The man hits his own huge chest with his fist.

He says, "This is me!"

"Oh. Well," says Hawkeye, backing away. "I guess that's sufficient."

A PLEA

Begin. Then go on.

What I've tried to say here is that spiritual study and practice take one through physiology and psychology, the body and the ego, through to a central understanding. And then they take one out the

other side with a very different perspective on living (and on dying).
To stop short of completing that journey, stuck in some quietening
condition of personal ease, or temporary relief, is to miss the point
of it all. It is to miss the real Homecoming.

This is how I understand spiritual study and practice at this
moment.

SABBATH CONSCIOUSNESS

Beatrice Bruteau

INTRODUCTION

Holy Saturday is in every way a Nothing Day. There is no liturgical celebration. The churches are empty. The altars are stripped. The tabernacles have been vacated, and their doors stand ajar. Nothing whatever is happening. What does this mean?

It is the Great Sabbath . . . the Great Silence, the Great Nothing that precedes the Feast of Redemption, of liberation from slavery and imprisonment, of entry into the new life of freedom.

To begin to appreciate it, to experience and savor it, we need to understand the significance of the Sabbath in general. It is, no doubt, an endless study, for not only have scholars thought about it for thousands of years, but worshippers commit themselves to live it and experience it deeper and deeper throughout their lives.

Sabbath comes from the Hebrew word for *rest*. It recalls the Creation and God's rest when it was completed. It is characterized by cessation of creative physical activity. "God blessed the seventh day and hallowed it because on it, God rested from all his work which he had done in creation" (Genesis 2:3). We in turn are commanded, "Observe the Sabbath day to keep it holy. Six days you shall labor and do all your work, but the seventh day is a Sabbath to the Lord your God. In it you shall not do any work" (Deuteronomy 5:12–13). Notice that sabbath observance is not just a practical and sensible and compassionate practice, but it is a way of relating to the holiness of God and of entering into the secret of divine life.

I want to develop three thoughts on this subject. One has to do with not laboring, another with holiness and wholeness, and these I will treat briefly. The third has to do with formlessness and nothingness, and this I will say more about. They all have to do with consciousness.

By "consciousness" I mean our interior sense of ourselves and of the whole of whatever we know as reality. It is the basic and generic act of awareness, which is the condition for the exercise of particular interior activities that result in patterning this awareness. The patterns include our general orientation or mind-set, our beliefs, attitudes, feelings, conceptual systems, ways of thinking and judging, our desires and volitions. I contrast two fundamental patternings and positionings of our intentional life: ordinary consciousness, by which I mean the beliefs, thoughts, and feelings that orientate us to the world of finite and relative things and to our work toward achievements; and what I am calling "sabbath consciousness," an interior orientation based on insight into the reality of the infinite and the nondual realization of our deep-rootedness in it.

NOT LABORING

In sabbath consciousness we do not have to rush or accomplish or produce. In sabbath consciousness we are not to labor. Labor is what is done on the six days, that is, in the finite and temporal world. It consists of moving things in relation to one another with a view to producing something, accomplishing something by our efforts. We exercise our natural talents and abilities and energies on the things of this world. And in terms of the spiritual life—the contemplative life—we exercise our natural spiritual talents of intelligence and goodwill and affectivity. Labor means trying to get closer to God by *doing things*, both exteriorly and interiorly.

But all that these spiritual exercises do is convince us that they are both impotent and unnecessary. They will not "produce" union with God, and they do not have to; our being united with God is something God does, not something we do—or, better, we are always united with God and cannot not be.

It is instructive to notice how our minds tend to work in a situation like this. When we find that we cannot cause the realization of union with God, we fly to the opposite extreme and assert that God causes it. But we seldom think to question whether it is caused at all; whether "causing" is a good category or aspect under which to consider this matter in the first place. We may not notice that both the scenario in which we bring about our union with God and the scenario in which God brings it about make the same assumption: that initially we and God are separated and must "pass to" a state of being united. This is a method we use in many instances: Forsake one pole of a duality and adhere to the opposite.

But spiritual insight comes about when we enter upon a further dimension: when we view from a nondual perspective; when we view orthogonally to the plane in which both those opposites lie.

Very often, this further dimension, which transcends both poles of the earlier opposition, will not have readily available language in which to express itself. This is why the mystics struggle so to invent metaphors and similes and parables that will somehow convey what they have experienced and understood.

So it is with sabbath consciousness. We must labor all these six days in order to break out of the consciousness that believes in the necessity and efficacy of such labor. "But the seventh day is a Sabbath to the Lord your God; in it you shall not do any work." It is God's Sabbath and therefore your Sabbath.

Saint Teresa of Ávila likens the spiritual life to tending a garden. The gardener labors in various ways to bring water to the garden, from carrying water by the pailful to diverting river water through irrigation channels, but in the end, all that is bypassed when it rains. This is the ultimate truth about our spiritual life, about our prayer life. It is not our labors, represented by the six days of work, that produce contemplative prayer or realization of divine union. Real prayer is present in God's Sabbath.

A certain part of our consciousness already knows this and can rest in this knowledge, even while we continue with our secular and spiritual labors. The attitude of sabbath rest is the attitude of confidence that trusts in the commandment to keep the Sabbath and to rest in it, and therefore not to identify one's deepest reality with the works and labors in which one engages.

What we call the commandments—sacred obligations—are really statements of revelation and empowerment. They are promises. They tell us what we need to know and to do in order to fulfill ourselves, and they promise that we are able to do what they say. This one says that we can keep the Sabbath of God's rest without labor and without break, that is, in wholeness, or holiness.

What does it mean to keep the Sabbath whole, without break? It means to rest our central consciousness steadily, without wavering, on God, the Wholeness, the Holy One, the Eternal. "Thou dost keep him in perfect peace whose mind is stayed on Thee" (Isaiah 26:3). This is the contemplative state. This is the same as "praying without ceasing." This is coming into realization of the truth that is the transcendent wholeness, the ultimate unity.

Too often our experience of our life is a fragmented experience. Yet we know, if we have any acquaintance with the spiritual life, even if only by hearsay—that is, by the traditional teachings and scriptures—that the underlying reality is a continuous wholeness, a unity beyond any possibility of division. This is part of the insight of monotheism in the Abrahamic religions and is, in that personalist context, represented dramatically as God's loyalty. God's will does not change. God is steadfast love. God's love, God's will, God's personal selfhood is one wholeness, unfragmented. A fragmented will can be loyal one day and defect the next. A fragmented will can change over time. But God's will is integral, utterly reliable, immovable, eternal. It means that God will never forsake us. "For His great love is without end," says Psalm 117, and 118 adds, "The faithfulness of God endures forever."

We are called to realize ourselves as children of God. Our will is to be the match and image of God's will: steadfast, without fluctuation, loyal, committed. If the will is focused in unity, then the rest of our life will be less fragmented. We will gradually draw all fragmentation back into original unity; we will experience what some Jewish mystics have called "reintegration." It is the achievement of that higher unity-penetrating diversity by which our own wholeness images the wholeness of God.

The Sabbath, in Jewish mysticism, is not a finite and relative form. It is the image and the consort of the invisible, the formless God. The formlessness of God is a very important truth. God is the infinite, the Absolute Being, having no name but I AM. The Sabbath, in Jewish sacred lore, is spoken of as the bride of God and queen. The union of God with his bride, the Sabbath, is the Jewish mystic's way of pointing to the wholeness of the Absolute. Christians might call it a "sacrament." The Sabbath represents God's eternity and enables the worshipper who takes it seriously to enter into the reality of which it is an external sign.

All sacraments enable human beings to contact a reality that is *always present*, although the sacrament itself stands apart from everyday experience in order to call attention to itself and to the reality that it mediates. Thus the Sabbath is not really one time among other times, but rather the underlying eternity, which *is* "all the time."

The deepest part of our consciousness knows that we live in eternity, that sabbath consciousness is the underlying, nondual consciousness on which the six working days develop their finite and relative forms. Only the Infinite, the Formless, can ground all forms. Sabbath consciousness is formless, like the God to whom it is united. This is why it is characterized by the cessation of works. It is not doing anything; it is not even being any particular kind of thing; it is just Being Itself. The works of motion and manifestation are withdrawn, called back into the abyss of the godhead, into invisibility.

HOLINESS AND WHOLENESS

Now I want to approach Holy Saturday from a slightly different angle, from Good Friday and what I will call "the death of the Word."

The central idea is that the mystical death is the death of all concepts—that is, the transcendence of all concepts because none of them is really adequate to the Infinite. The Creator-Word of the prologue of the gospel of John, the "singly generated God" that comes forth from the emptiness of the Father-Ground and "exegetes" the Invisible One, is now withdrawn back into that source from which it came (John 1:18).

In John 16:28 the Word says, "I came from the Father and have come into the world; again, I am leaving the world and going to the Father." This is the experience that is the passage for us to sabbath consciousness and its promise.

For contemplatives, this is now the heart of the matter. We are entering into the mystical night: the night in which "no one can work"; in which no one *need* work; in which the operations of human nature are transcended; in which the last vestiges of the isolated self are removed. The isolated self is the self that believes itself to be separate and set apart from others because it has wrapped itself in descriptions to give an appearance of distinctiveness. Thomas Merton says: "I wind experiences around myself and cover myself with pleasures and glory like bandages in order to make myself perceptible to myself and the world, as if I were an invisible body that could only become visible when something visible covered its surface."

At this stage in our spiritual journey, these coverings and disguises are stripped from us. You might say that the real self then shows. Or you might say that what is revealed is indeed the invisibility that is at our core. And saying that, you might remember that God is invisible and that we are children of God.

What does invisibility mean? I am equating it here with nakedness, and equating both nakedness and invisibility with ultimate reality. It means that ultimate reality cannot be conceived. We cannot form any idea of ultimate reality, in God or in ourselves, because there is nothing in terms of which to describe it, nothing to liken it to, and especially, nothing to contrast it with. God is "all in all." There is no non-God. As the psalmist says, there is no place you can go to get away from God; the divine Presence is everywhere. As there is nothing to contrast with God, there is nothing against which God can be perceived as a figure against a ground. God cannot be one thing rather than another. God is the Ultimate Ground.

But each word picks out something from the general sea of reality and directs attention to that something. Any particular word we might choose would have to ignore something by directing attention to its meaning rather than some other meaning. And all words are representational; they represent realities. As the incarnate Word says repeatedly, "I have not spoken on my own authority; the Father who sent me has . . . given me commandment what to say and what to speak. . . . What I say therefore I say as the Father has bidden me. . . . The words that I say to you I do not speak on my own authority; but the Father who dwells in me does his works" (John 12:50, 14:10). So, although the way to the Source is through the Word, the Word itself is not the Source and at the last moment has to be withdrawn.

This stage of the spiritual journey is often called "the dark night of the soul." This does not mean some kind of depression or sorrow or despair. It is parallel to "the dark night of the senses" and means that those faculties have, so to speak, turned off. Significant information—for our spiritual purposes—no longer comes to us from our sense life when we cease building our lives around sense experiences. This is what happens in the early days of the spiritual journey when our major interest shifts from the pleasures of the senses to affairs of the spirit.

Now we enter into the night of the soul as well, when the faculties of the mind no longer can provide us with significant information for our spiritual purposes. It is not that our intellect is too weak for the mystery and magnitude of God. It is rather that the reality we are now touching, or entering, is *formless*. It is by definition inaccessible to the faculty for perceiving and judging forms. When all the limiting forms that cannot describe the Ultimate Ground have been abandoned, only the naked invisibility of God is left.

Since knowing, as we have been used to practicing knowing, no longer works, we must go by way of unknowing. But we can still be conscious in this way because we are now much more in the very source of consciousness: consciousness *prior* to its limitation by the various forms. Here is to be found the glory we had before the foundation of the world. Instead of looking at, which requires comparison or the contrast of a figure against a ground, we simply coincide—consciously—with that in which we cognitively rest.

The author of *The Cloud of Unknowing* also wrote *The Book of Privy Counsel*, in which this instruction for prayer at this stage is given:

> Offer up your naked, blind feeling of your own being. And, as I often say, always take care that it is naked, and not clothed by any quality of your being . . . or with any other special condition proper to man's being rather than to the being of other created things.
>
> You must have no more regard for the qualities of God's being than for the qualities of your own

being. For there is no name nor feeling nor regard which agrees better, nor even so well, with eternity, which God is, as does that which may be had and seen and felt in the blind and loving regard of this word *is*.

This nakedness is an image of the return to the source, the beginning of the world, as well as the end of the world; the withdrawal of the creative Word in which all the finite forms appear. By intentional nakedness, we have come back to where we began, the point at which we came straight from the heart of God, pure as our Creator.

In the traditional story, Adam and Eve, the archetypes of humanity, are "naked" and "not ashamed." Of course not. As there was nothing to gain, and nothing to defend, so there was nothing to hide. Why should there be? All that traffic in appearances came later, after ingestion of the fruit of knowledge and judgment according to categories of "good" and "evil." This is not a historical account, not a chronological sequence. This story is saying that at the center of our reality is this original purity, overlaid by the polarities of appearance-experience.

When we return, through contemplative practice, to the condition of the beginning, we become again "as little children," as those who come naked from their mother's womb. You remember that this was the response of Job, when he was stripped of all his possessions, of all that made his social life meaningful. He worshipped God and said, "Naked I came from my mother's womb, and naked shall I return" (Job 1:21). This saying is echoed in Ecclesiastes (5:15): "As he came from his mother's womb, he shall go again, naked as he came, and shall take nothing for his toil which he may carry away in his hand." This text also says that toil is useless. We simply abandon all works by which we had built up our sense of embodied self.

Michael von Brück, in *The Unity of Reality*, summarizes the prayer method recommended by the author of *The Cloud of Unknowing* (I'll paraphrase a bit here), whereby we are able to forget our usual sense of self:

> We enter a state of perfect spiritual calm quite naturally, once sense images have been abandoned and the content of our thoughts has ceased to exist thanks to concentration. The one who learns to harness the mind attains this emptiness, which is neither good nor bad in itself. We need not suppress distractions, but let them drop along the way to concentration, helped by the occasional repetition of the last words we can use: God, love, is. The emptiness receives its value from our motivation, our aspiration. Genuine mystical prayer is based on love-filled spiritual peace which God gives. Mystical experience is grace.

Just as God is Love, so God is Grace. We may think of grace as a thing, in contrast with another thing. But grace is the free and original gift of oneself, unprovoked, unmotivated, unrewarded. And this is the very life of God. So it is not exactly that God "gives" us grace, as an act that might or might not happen, or that we "receive" grace, as something rare or something that we do not deserve. Grace is beyond the kind of contrasting situations we set up in our descriptive thinking. Grace is beyond even subjects and objects and transitive actions. Grace is Divine Life.

A sense of the actions of God—the life of God—being "intransitive" seems to me to be helpful and important, though difficult to express. It has to do with going beyond that kind of consciousness in which we distinguish subject and object. For instance, we tend to say "I love God," or "God loves me." That's transitive; the subject acts on or toward the object and both are defined by this, that is, "finitized." But the real truth of the matter is that God is love. We may perhaps say "God loves . . ." but if so, there won't be any object, anything to set up in front of God. Similarly, we might say "God gives . . ." or we ourselves might say "I'm grateful." But there won't be any objects to complete those sentences. It's not said what God gives, or to whom. We don't say to whom we are grateful or for what. The experience is too big for that, too all-encompassing, and there is no sense of separation or dualism between one and the other; a transitive sense is not applicable.

Or we might explain that the experience—of gratitude, for instance—is too empty for transitives to be used. The bliss of the mystical realization is not a happiness *about* anything, and it is not even a pleasure as opposed to a pain. The ultimate state is never a condition of experiencing one pole of a pair of opposites.

You may wonder whether anyone actually experiences such a thing. But mystical literature is full of such descriptions. The senses are dead; the usual operations of the mind are suspended; and the "heart"—the core consciousness—is intensely awake in itself, in God.

Absolute bliss is that state which remains as ground when all the particular pleasures and pains have been withdrawn. Absolute being is that state which remains as ground when all the particular forms of being are withdrawn. Absolute consciousness is that state which remains as ground when all the particular objects of consciousness are withdrawn.

FORM AND FORMLESSNESS

Now we are at the heart of the Great Sabbath, the ground of all possibilities. To quote Franklin Merrell-Wolff, pure consciousness "is both the culmination and the beginning of all possibilities." But in order for the possibilities, the resurrection experiences, to have their proper value, we need to be sure that we have experienced the divine nothingness as deeply as we can.

This is why Holy Saturday, the Great Sabbath, is so important.

It is the day sacred to the invisibility of God, the day on which there is no motion, no manifestation. It alone in the Christian calendar represents, by its very lack of liturgy, the Unmanifest, the hidden God. Perhaps we may regard Holy Saturday, the Day of Sacred Nothingness, as commemorative of God the Formless, the Infinite.

Often people who have gone into the wilderness speak of "hearing the silence." When I go into the empty church on Holy Saturday (before the ceremonies of the Easter Vigil, which are supposed to take place late in the night), and when I experience the paradox of the holy nothingness reverberating, as it were, on all sides, it seems to me that we have here a powerful absence-presence of the Primeval One, whose Word has been called back into itself, whose manifestation is temporarily withdrawn, whose self-revelation is gathered into its own essential unity for the timeless moment of the Great Sabbath.

For the Jews, the Sabbath is the messianic moment, as the messianic time is called "the time of perpetual Sabbath." The messianic era is the time of peace and harmony, of union between man and God, man and man, and man and nature. It is a time of liberation from bondage. Therefore the Great Sabbath stands before the Passover, the festival of release and freedom.

Union between man and God, and release from bondage: I have some small thoughts on this.

I've said that the central point is the reconciliation of the finite and the infinite. The withdrawing of the Word is not an end in itself; that is, it is not *the* end. It is done so that we may refocus, having lost the idea of our separation from God or from each other. To do that, we have to unfocus first.

This withdrawal of the Word, or death, has to be done because of our sense of separation, of severalness-severedness, of local ego-self-reference, and the protection and aggrandizement and domination behaviors that result from that. Remember, this withdrawal or death is something that takes place in our own contemplative life. We are talking now about the interior mystical meaning of the traditional teachings. Our word use, belief in idea systems, reliance on concepts, has to die, be withdrawn, in order that the sense of separation may disappear, so that we may know union.

It has to be done when the time is right, when the hour has come for it to be done, and not sooner. That means when the local ego-consciousness has matured sufficiently. Having local ego-consciousness was not a mistake. We call it "sin," and suggest thereby that it ought not to be, but we are able to do this work only because we have matured enough in the moral order to deplore many of the things that our biological drive to survive, and our psychological sense of vulnerability and insufficiency, lead us to do to defend and augment our limited being. But it was necessary in order to create a finite world. You can't have a moral order without a psychological order, nor a psychological without a biological order. And "severalization" is necessary to create these orders of reality.

Differentiation has to be the beginning, and when the complexity has sufficiently advanced so that we have consciousness on the moral level and on the metaphysical level, and therefore are fit for the mystical level, then a kind of reversal in the process can be set in motion. You may be familiar with psychologists saying that you have to have an ego before you can overcome it, you have to have a secure self before you can undertake to be "selfless." What I am saying is similar, only generalized to the metaphysical level and applied mystically. This death of the Word is the necessary step at this point in the full project of God's creation.

The other small thought has to do with release from bondage. This means eventually some kind of cosmic transformation, but it also can be interpreted in our personal and psychological terms. When we have reached the mystical peak of the death of the Word, we are in "paradise." Paradise means the great bliss of being at the heart, being consciously in God, being at the foundation and core of all being, unity, truth, goodness, and beauty; being one's real Self, being enlightened, being free. It also means experiencing the liberating joy of realizing the divine, unconditional love. This makes us feel totally secure and completely fulfilled. It is the deep

Satisfaction (as Merrell-Wolf calls it) of this paradise experience that makes possible what happens next.

When we are deeply centered, when we have tasted the bliss of paradise, when we are thoroughly reassured and thus released, then a great transformation occurs in our depths.

All actions begin as consciousness-movements in the mind/heart. Prior to a deep enlightenment experience, many of these movements "do not obey." Trying to control them by sheer willpower, as St. Paul testifies, does not work. The will cannot take new actions until the spiritual perception–power gives it the insight from which to do them. As long as one's perspective is lined up in terms of local ego-centered reference and value, the will has to will in terms of that value as the ultimate good. That reference has to be changed first. Then the will can do the good, naturally and spontaneously. Commandments to control your behavior, rein-forced by sanctions, promises of rewards and punishments, are not the way to achieve transformation. You have to go down to the root and relieve whatever is imprisoned there. This is why Jesus is repre-sented as going down into Hell to set the prisoners free. And he does it by preaching the Good News—neither threats nor rewards—but Truth. When you can *know* that Truth, it will set you free.

It is the freeing power of the paradise experience that unlocks the gates of hell. The great relief we feel in the bliss of heaven makes it possible for us to let go the cramping, repressive restraints we had put on our prisoners. Because of the light and warmth of the divine unconditional love, these buried energies now have no need to protect or avenge themselves, to grieve or to hate, to run away or to strike. This is what happens in contemplative experience through the gradual dying away of the identification with particu-lars, the removal of the veils of the self, the passage from dualism to nondualism, the death of the Word, the entering into the Great Sabbath. This is what transforms and releases all the mature ener-gies of consciousness.

And here, finally, we become capable of conformation to the

will of God. When our perceptions have been purified, released, transformed, refocused, when we are no longer conceiving either ourselves or God in finite terms, then we become fit to enter into the will of God. Earlier, we might have interpreted the will of God either as something extremely distasteful to ourselves, or as something favorable, and therefore fated, for our group, nation, religion, or whatever.

Those are two very common mistakes made when people talk about the will of God. A third one comes up when people are trying to make decisions and they talk as if they are trying to second-guess God. We are not ready to relate sensibly to the will of God as long as we are identifying everything in terms of finite meanings and values, and pretty local ones at that. We have to become capable of seeing a much larger picture first.

We have to be able to coincide with a God who "makes the sun to rise on the evil and on the good, and sends rain on the just and on the unjust" (Matthew 5:45). When we begin to grasp the scale and the generosity—the unconditionality—of it, then we can say meaningfully "May your kingdom come, your will be done on earth as it is in heaven."

CONCLUSION

This, it seems to me, is the halfway mark of what our revelatory tradition is telling us. Withdrawing from the dispersed and objectified, externally projected consciousness, into the central unity through the death of the Word, we find sabbath rest in the ultimate ground. We stop seeing conditions and boundaries and separations. It is important to do this right, and as thoroughly as we can, because we are now going to put the multiplicity and particularity back. When we do, it has to be done from this experienced root in the sabbath ground. We go into the sabbath rest of pure being by way of emptying consciousness and by the death of concepts. We come out again in resurrection, by way of goodness and beauty, on the first day of a new working week, wearing again the seamless garment, woven as one from top to bottom, which was always ours and was never torn, throughout all our experiences.

I want to emphasize that this is something that can be done in this life, as Jesus made plain to Martha. It is not postponed to some vague end of the world, but is here and now in the resurrection life of the I AM. It may be difficult to do, but it is not impossible. It's not a question of biological functioning but of consciousness functioning. It is being able to see both things at once, the unity and the multiplicity, the infinite and the finite, the absolute and the relative, the transcendent and the cosmic. See them as reconciled, not mutually exclusive; see them as nondual, as concretized in the great cosmic incarnation in which we take part.

Holy Saturday, then, may be said to stand at the peak of the liturgical year. It is not a mere stage wait between two acts of the liturgical drama but is itself the climax and the crisis, the turning point. It represents, on the one hand, the withdrawal of the Manifestation and the absolute hiddenness and nothingness of God the Source. And on the other hand, or as a consequence of the first, it represents the new world, the kingdom of God, in which there is no labor, or struggle of beings against one another, or fragmentation and alienation, but rather integration and wholeness, with love and beauty reigning supreme. Holy Saturday is the pinnacle of the contemplative's quest for union with God, and the beginning of the contemplative's task, the redemption of the world.

This essay was adapted from the third talk in a series, given at the 14th General Assembly of the Association of Contemplative Sisters, Catherine Spalding Center, Nazareth, Kentucky, July 27–August 2, 1994. For further reading on this topic see Bruteau's essay in *New Blackfriars* magazine (Oxford, England, March 1990), and her books, *Radical Optimism* (New York: Crossroad, 1993), and *The Easter Mysteries* (New York: Crossroad, 1995).

HIDDEN IN THE PRESENT

Annabeth McCorkle

"QUICK NOW, HERE, NOW, ALWAYS—"

Axiomatic to the idea and practice of spiritual work is the sense that our ordinary awareness is limited. The world as usually perceived is not the whole story. There is something—Something of Great Value—that is hidden or lost or forgotten. Our destiny and our desire is to find it.

All traditions suggest that the *hidden* is really only the *unnoticed*. What's needed to make the invisible visible is a shift of perspective toward what has been here all the time. This is the paradox of "the gateless gate" and "the open secret."

The literature of the spiritual traditions abounds with allegorical stories of lost treasures, where they are found, and the toils and hardships required to find them. A retelling of a Hasidic story goes like this.

Isaac was very poor, so poor that he didn't have even the simple necessities of life. One night he dreamed that he would find a great treasure under a certain bridge in a distant city. At first Isaac ignored the dream, but when it came to him for the third time, he packed a shovel and a few belongings and set out. After many days, he arrived at the bridge he had dreamed about only to find that it was under constant surveillance by the king's guardsmen. There was no way to dig for the treasure. Even so, the next day and the day after and the day after that and the day after that, Isaac went to the bridge and, from sunrise to sunset, wandered over and around and under the bridge. One day, the captain of the guards, who had been watching Isaac, asked him what he was looking for. Isaac told him about his poverty and about his dream. The captain laughed and said, "Ah, dreams! If I believed my dreams, I would have gone to your town to look for a treasure under the stove in a house of a Jew named Isaac." Then he laughed again. After bowing to the captain, Isaac traveled back to his own town and his own home, where he dug up the treasure from under his own stove. In gratitude, Isaac built a house of prayer.

When Martin Buber relates his version of the story he says, "Rabbi Bunam used to add: 'There is something you cannot find anywhere in the world, not even at the zaddik's, and there is, nevertheless, a place where you can find it.' " Uri Shulevitz concludes *The Treasure*, his rendering of the story in a children's picture book, with "Sometimes one must travel far to discover what is near."

The treasure is hidden in our own home. The Kingdom of God is within us, and until we find it, we will never be at peace. Saint Augustine says,

> *Thou has made us for Yourself, O Lord,*
> *And our hearts are restless*
> *'Til they rest in Thee.*

These words refer to what could be called "the inner imperative": a need that is both a call from and a response to another level of being. This inner imperative may be experienced directly, or as a wordless yearning, or as a sense that "all is not right, yet there is

Rightness." Sometimes mere whispers from another realm seep into
the mind as existential questions: "What is true? What's the meaning and purpose of life? Who am I? Do I have a part to play?"

The fulfillment of the inner imperative requires nothing less
than a radical change of being. It will not happen by chance; it
requires specific and, as is said, lawful efforts over a long period of
time. This leads some people to connect themselves with a genuine
spiritual tradition: a system of inner development whose purpose is,
as Michel de Salzmann says, "self-realization and the development
of corresponding capacities for manifestation."

GUIDE AND STUDENT

The transmission of the teaching is the primary function of a
spiritual guide. He does this in a number of ways: directly by his
presence; by oral and written words; and by what could be called
"the forms" (or vehicles) of the tradition—inner practices, exercises,
prayers, sacred dance, chanting, music, sitting, and rituals. If the
seeker actively engages with these forms, they become a bridge that
leads back to the teaching's source where understanding replaces
knowledge.

Of a genuine spiritual guide it could be said: "There is a stage
of development where detachment and compassion, like eternity
and time, are not incompatible," to use William Segal's words. The
guide assists others to realize their possibility of, as Gurdjieff says,
"becoming particles of the whole of the 'Reasonable Whole.'"

Spiritual guides come with differing degrees of insight and
development: teacher, advisor, more experienced student. What's
important is that she has trod the path, paid the price, and knows
what's what. The guide creates conditions in which the student can
begin her own search within the context of a proven system of
inner work, which includes a movement from outer teacher to inner
teacher to all the world as teacher.

In recent years, ornithologists have been concerned about the loss of the natural environment along the paths of certain migratory birds. The information about the migration patterns, generally passed down from generation to generation, is being lost in some endangered species. Could migratory birds be retaught the routes by migrating with people? In the fall of 1993, Bill Lishman, piloting an ultralight aircraft (resembling a large noisy bird more than an airplane), successfully led eighteen Canada geese from Canada to Virginia. The next year thirty-eight geese followed him to South Carolina. The flights were deemed successful when the birds returned to Canada the following spring without assistance.

The metaphor is not exact, but there is a similarity between the relationship of guide and student and the relationship of Lishman and the geese. The students and the geese are without the knowledge of the route home. They follow the direction indicated by someone who knows, but everyone has to flap his own wings to get there. There are no free flights. Having made the trip there and back once, they have to find how to repeat the journey again and again by themselves.

For many people, the relationship between guide and student doesn't come easily. Along with his inner imperative, the student has unconscious expectations about the guide, expectations relating to authority figures: desires, fears, and coping skills. Having seen himself, the guide knows the student as well. The guide remembers why the student came to this work, even when the student himself has forgotten. Using "skillful means," he enters into the student's condition just enough to draw him out without getting drawn in himself.

There's a Buddhist story about a group of children trapped in a burning house. The children, intent on playing and telling each other stories, are unaware of the danger around them. Their parents cry, "Children, drop what you are doing. The house is on fire. Come out." But the children are interested only in their games and do not budge from their spot. A wise man passing by sees the children and calls out to them, "Look, children, see what I have. Toys. Lots of toys, wonderful toys. Come out of the house so you can

play with them." Lured by the promise of the toys, the children
come out of the burning house. Only then do they understand the
nature of the situation.

THE KEY

We've considered the inner imperative and the need for the
help and support offered by a genuine tradition. We've looked at
the guide's function and relationship to the student. Now let's
return to the matter of "the hidden." Where and how can it be
"found"?

In a well-known Sufi story, a friend finds Mulla Nassr Eddin
on his hands and knees on the road under a streetlamp on a dark
night. "What are you looking for?" the friend asks. "My house
key," the mulla replies. The friend joins the mulla, and they scour
the ground together but without success. After a time, the friend
asks, "Where exactly did you lose your key?" "Over there," says
the mulla, pointing into the shadows where the illumination of the
streetlamp doesn't reach. "Then why are you looking here?" asks
the friend. The mulla replies, "Because the light is better."

What the mulla really wants is to get into his house. He hasn't
lost the house. He's lost the key to get into it, and he's looking for
that in the wrong place. The mulla and we are the same.

Our house isn't lost. The Tao hasn't abandoned us. God isn't
dead. What we seek is hidden in the present, waiting to be found.
Our predicament is that we aren't in conscious contact with it, and
we've lost the experiential knowledge of where and how to regain
it. We need a key to get in.

There is much confusion around this point. We haven't lost
contact with the "idea" of Ultimate Reality. It's talked about all the
time, often by people with little experience of real inner work.
People who really know something are usually reluctant to speak
about "what will be found," lest it interfere with another person's
own search.

There are always people who say the key is "Do as I say" or "Believe as I tell you." Accepting someone else's truth (or idea of truth) is no answer at all. A man's stomach isn't filled by licking another man's plate. The person with the inner imperative must discover for himself. He'll never be content with secondhand truth.

The lost key is attention: the capacity for seeing, for noticing, for being aware. This capacity is separate from the object of seeing, noticing, being aware.

What we seek is in the present: the everpresent present, the interior present. Attention is the key that, by turning, unlocks the door to what we seek. So—we study attention.

ATTENTION

Is there an experience of attention that is independent of our ideas of what attention is? Where is the attention right now? What does it mean to pay attention? How is the attention habitually and automatically drawn away? Is there a subtle inner gesture that permits it or induces it to stay here? Are there different levels or qualities of attention?

We've said that the inner imperative is about a radical change of being. It has nothing to do with attempts to fix the system according to our own "specs," which are often just a reshuffling of subjective material all on the same level. In contrast, the spiritual traditions are about a complete overhaul: a retooling of a twelve-volt system to accommodate high-voltage. To mix a few more metaphors, it's about plugging the leaks, dredging the canal, widening the pipes, and opening the dikes.

In this we have a small and absolutely necessary part to play, but we ourselves are not the agents of change. What's up to us is an intentional work of attention, at once inward and outward, toward the present moment. The spiritual practices and forms of a tradition, although initially seen as more related to actions of the body and the intellect, support the movement of the attention back into the present. The real inner work is simply a search for an attention that plumbs the depth and breadth of the present. This could be called "attentiveness practice."

Attentiveness practice involves an active search for the right effort to bring the attention here, now. It is the paradoxical "effort-less effort" that is best described by what it's not. It is neither non-effort ("effortless effortlessness") nor a forceful push or strain to get somewhere or find something or make something happen. There's no "doing" to, or of, attention. What exactly is the effort? This is our search.

Although the head has a part to play, the effort is not an action of the intellect. Thinking about attentiveness practice is not the right effort. Attentiveness practice does not develop as a logical progression. On the contrary, attentiveness practice reveals the essential discontinuity between levels of being.

There is a natural distinction between the imperatives of life that occupy much of our faculties and attention and the inner imperative. This has led to an illusory dichotomy between body and spirit. This misunderstanding has hindered the necessary explo-ration of the body's role in spiritual transformation.

When we first undertake to bring the attention into the present and keep it here, we are struck by the enormous difficulty of the effort. We don't remember to try, and when we do, we can't sustain the effort for long. The mind wishes, but it is not enough. The heart must wish too.

A staying power has to be developed.

Also to be developed is a capacity for uncertainty and unknow-ingness, as well as a tolerance for discomfort and unableness.

PRACTICE

Attentiveness practice begins with a simple noticing accompa-nied by an awareness of the noticing. This includes an attentive-ness to myself, to what spiritual teachers have called "the creature," "the machine," "the body-mind complex," and "this person." Each reaction to what is seen can become the next thing noticed—layer after layer after layer. As attentiveness practice deepens, the attention disengages from the myriad layers of debris from the past, gathers itself in the present, and gradually is liberated from the tensions and effects of the fundamental illusion of identity.

Through attentiveness practice we see ourselves. We find that our ordinary attention is partial, in both the usual meanings of the word: being in parts or unwhole, and having preferences for this or that. The attention is scattered, only partially present even to our ordinary life. The attention is conditioned to a preference to see and experience only certain things.

What's called for is an impartial attention of a quality capable of embracing the whole without preference.

What we see contrasts sharply, and sometimes painfully, with our *ideas* of how things are or should be. Things happen not at all the way we think they do. Our capabilities and powers for doing, controlling, and understanding are considerably less than we imagined. Over the years, we have worked quite hard, primarily unconsciously, to avoid these uncomfortable truths.

OBSTACLES

We realize that "a man's foes shall be they of his own household" (Matthew 10:36). Everything is in us.

Besides the inner imperative and the imperatives of life, there is a "me" imperative, which has nothing to do with a healthy psyche for effective and meaningful life in the world. There is a preference for "this form that goes by the name of (fill in the blank)." From one point of view, it doesn't matter whether these impulses are manifested through actions or not. We need to develop a tolerance for the innocent but unpleasant stench of ourselves.

All traditions have named the obstacles encountered on the spiritual path. The early Christian fathers identified Seven Deadly Sins (pride, avarice, lust, anger, gluttony, envy, and sloth). The Buddhists enumerated the Ten Fetters (delusion of self, doubt, belief in the efficacy of ceremonies and ritual, sensuality, ill-will, passion for earthly life, desire for future life, pride, self-righteousness, and ignorance). The Old Testament recorded Ten Commandments, beginning with "Thou shalt have no other gods before me." Gurdjieff named (besides an extensive list of the forms of egoism) "self-calming, the disease tomorrow, suggestibility, indignation at the defects of others, a tendency to put other people on the right path, the calm self-contentment in the use of that which is not personally deserved, and the urge to become free from the necessity of actualizing the being-efforts demanded by Nature."

Confirmation that the sins of the world are in me is not cause for shame. This conditioned emotion serves only to reinforce the idea of an isolated and embattled "me," which is the source of the sins to begin with. Recognition that the sins are common to all people is no consolation. Rather, there emerges in some people a feeling of deep grief that, as Gurdjieff says, "on account of the undesirable elements present in them, they are still unable to help HIM in the fulfillment of HIS most sacred tasks for the good of our whole Megalocosmos." The intentional experiencing of this sorrow has a transformative power.

In the early Christian Orthodox Church, the ascetic monks were required to reveal their most private thoughts and feelings to their spiritual advisor. Done rightly, this could bring the monastic toward what Gurdjieff calls "impartial self-observation." The monks' method will never pass muster in these times, but perhaps there is something to learn from it. Could we find, with Pourrat, "a total confidence in the opening of the heart to a superior to the point where one reveals even one's most secret thoughts to him"? Perhaps to an inner superior?

T. S. Eliot writes, in "East Coker":

Shall I say it again? In order to arrive there,
To arrive where you are, to get from where you are not,
*   You must go by a way wherein there is no ecstasy.*

In order to arrive at what you do not know
You must go by a way which is the way of ignorance.
In order to possess what you do not possess
You must go by the way of dispossession.
In order to arrive at what you are not
You must go through the way in which you are not.
And what you do not know is the only thing you know
And what you own is what you do not own
And where you are is where you are not.

This morning, I am carrying two dishes across the dining porch to feed our dog Thorfinn. As I approach the door, I set one dish on top of the other in order to free one hand to turn the door handle. In one moment, I know that the upper dish is unstable. In the next moment, it falls to the floor splattering dog food, water, and raw egg all over the rug. I wave away offers of help to clean up the mess. I call Thorfinn inside to let him eat his breakfast and clean the rug at the same time. He appears perplexed. He looks oddly at the mess and then at me as if to say, "This isn't where I usually eat, yet it is my food." After a short pause, he begins to eat.

We eat our food wherever we find it, even if it isn't in the usual or preferred place.

Spiritual work rattles the cage of our prison. Jesus says, "Think not that I am come to send peace on earth" (Matthew 10:34). Willingly accepted difficulty and friction are necessary in the hand-in-hand process of disillusionment and realization: losing our illusions and making real the truth. Sometimes there is great value in desperation. Unexpected or unpleasant conditions can disturb our psychic slumber. "Impossible" or "intolerable" situations, to which we can find no satisfactory resolution in the usual ways, can bring us right to the brink where they can be transformed into the next note in the song of our work.

Louise March said of her teacher, Gurdjieff:

He did not wish simply to give new verbal knowledge. He wanted to change, open, develop something in the essence of man, which could lead him to the creation of his own inner world and give him understanding. Gurdjieff knew that anything of value has to be worked for. He never gave the teaching in an easily accessible form but always "buried the bone deeper."

EXPERIENCE

Life with its disease, death, suffering, ill-will, injustice, beauty, sacrifice, regeneration, love, and playfulness is one great enigma. The forms of the spiritual traditions, particularly practices, koans, and Gurdjieff's movements, make a demand that exceeds "my" capacity. Nothing short of real change can meet the demand.

Spiritual pondering, that is, intentionally carrying a "how?" or "what?" question unrelated to our personal lives, presents a unique opportunity to be precise. Quiet. A shift of direction. Presentation of the question toward the inner oracle. Attention momentarily steady. A crack in the shell. A fleeting glimpse of a direction. An attempt to formulate what is seen. Now the difficulty of precision because the contact is broken. How to be here at the point of the entry of an impression from another level?

Not all questions are the same. Sometimes by subjecting ourselves to questions or paradoxes that can't be resolved by conceptual thought, we realize we've been asking the wrong question; there's a faulty assumption embedded in the question itself.

When we were small children learning to walk, we unconsciously factored in the force of gravity. What other assumptions have been factored into our lives? Have we even assumed a mistaken identity? Is this why it's nearly impossible to entertain a real question about identity? If we could cease "striving to be not what one is," as Gurdjieff says, would we discover who we are?

The alarm clock rings at five o'clock this Easter morning. Through the bedroom window a full moon shines in the dark western sky. By the time I am out of the shower, the moon has dropped behind the neighbor's trees. After a short drive, my husband and I arrive at our community's country property. It's 6:15 A.M., time for the sun's scheduled appearance in Upstate New York today. In front of the new building, thirty people, singly and in small groups, stand facing east in the cold, clear morning. We join them. Minute by minute the eastern sky lightens, but no sun appears. Behind us, the full moon is reflected in the pond. Slowly the moon moves toward the western horizon. The eastern sky becomes pink and golden. Time passes as we stand in the cold. Silence reigns except for the ever-enlarging chorus of birdsong: sweet voices, chirps, cheeps, tweets, trills, clucks, coos, and quacks. More time passes. Aware of the body, the cold. Enduring with willingness. The thought arises, "Maybe the sun won't rise today!" Just as the moon disappears below the western horizon, the sun appears above the eastern horizon. We stand awhile longer until the round sun is fully visible.

When the moon sets, the sun rises. When self is forgotten, Self is remembered.

In *Tricycle: The Buddhist Review*, Thich Nhat Hanh speaks of two kinds of Buddhism: popular Buddhism and deep Buddhism. He says, "Which kind of Buddhism you're talking about is very important. It requires learning and practice, because anything you say in the second may be misunderstood and can create damage."

This brings up an idea not popular in our supposedly egalitarian society: esotericism. We live at a time when feelings of "self-esteem" are much esteemed. There's an inclination to explain everything in terms of what is already known or has been experienced and a tendency to reduce the most sublime of experiences to the service of our ordinary lives. However, the spiritual traditions are based on a knowledge that, though available to all, is apprehended by only a few. Gesshin Midwer, a Zen priest, says, "There are no secret teachings, only secret ears."

Many people value the taste of a life touched by results of

attentiveness practice, but only some are capable of, or interested
in, the level and intensity of inner work that's required for a radical
change of being. Few people embrace the inner teaching fully by
following the advice formulated by Gurdjieff: "If you go on a spree
then go the whole hog including the postage." Some people work
to partake of the fruit of the tree, and some will be satisfied with
nothing less than the tree. Roshi Philip Kapleau said in an interview
in *Tricycle:*

> My own experience of almost thirty years
> teaches me that there are very few people who have
> the kind of do-or-die aspiration necessary to
> achieve awakening. I don't think that is entirely tied
> to our insistence on comfort. Americans have, even
> in modern times, done some pretty heroic things
> and have undergone suffering for the sake of oth-
> ers. So, that kind of determination is there. The
> preparation for the arousal of it—the training—has
> not been fully developed.

While acknowledging the relative rarity and significance of the
genuine esoteric experience, caution in this matter is well advised.
Genuine spiritual work is not about a single experience—or a hundred experiences. It's a way of life, a path without end. Furthermore, esotericism doesn't imply elitism, which is a system of
judgment, exclusion, and arrogance.

People join a spiritual community for a variety of reasons.
Many come with a sense that life has a purpose beyond their personal lives, and they follow the teaching the best they can. Some
people connect themselves to a spiritual tradition to become more
psychologically or physically healthy, or to become a better person
in order to help the world, or to be a member of a supportive community, or to enrich their children's lives with a system of beliefs
and morality.

Within a spiritual community, everyone, regardless of his or her level of aspiration or development, is an expression of all that exists in this moment. Then everyone can help and be helped.

Several years ago, we bought a hummingbird feeder: a glass cylinder with a long narrow tube, which we filled with a prepared sugar-water solution designed especially for hummingbirds. Almost as soon as we hung the apparatus outside, honeybees swarmed over it. They drank all the sweet solution, so when the hummingbirds came, there was nothing left. Eventually we threw the feeder away. This year I am given another hummingbird feeder but with an additional component, a rubber "bee guard" that permits only hummingbirds to feed on the fine sweet liquid meant for them.

The operative words in this matter are inclusion and exchange. And then what must be protected will be protected. There is a need to sound one's own note but also to hear the whole melody.

The hand is extended with the fingers pointing outward. Each finger is identified by name: thumb, index finger, middle finger, fourth finger, little finger. Each finger defines itself partially— exclusively as that finger. Each finger notices characteristics that distinguish it from the other fingers. The thumb has only one joint but is involved in every activity of the fingers. The fourth finger is adorned, either deservedly or undeservedly, with a gold ring. The index finger has a special relationship with the thumb. The little finger is pretty but not very strong. The third finger is tall. The fingers have been told that each of these traits is better or worse than others.

An enlargement of perspective brings a moment of insight: "We're all fingers despite the subjective differences. Unique and wonderful." A larger vision reveals: "It's all hand."

The maturation of inner work is an inclusive life lived both as finger with other fingers and as hand. The hand and the fingers are one. If a single finger disturbs, it is not cut off but rehabilitated. Helping the fingers helps the hand.

Sometimes the small daily events of our lives shape themselves into stories that indicate a congruence of similar things on different scales.

Our children are hunting for their Easter baskets this morning. As usual, we've hidden the baskets, each labeled with a child's name, in plain sight somewhere in the house. They don't need to touch or move anything to discover their own basket. By standing in a different part of the house, by bending over, looking behind, or peering under, five of the six children claim their rewards. One child remains; he can't find his basket anywhere. Everyone else sees it. The rest of us help with clues. "Colder." "Warmer." "It's on the first floor." "It's in the dining room." He looks under the table, on the buffet, inside the china cabinet, on the windowsill behind the drapes, and on the seat of each chair tucked under the table. He begins to doubt that it's really here. We shout encouragement: "Keep looking." He has looked under, around, beneath, but now, as if called by the basket itself, he looks up. Here it is. The basket hangs by its handle from an arm of the chandelier. In plain sight.

Quick now, here, now, always—
A condition of complete simplicity
(Costing not less than everything).

JEWISH SPIRITUALITY— GUIDELINES FOR THE STILL PERPLEXED

Laura Bernstein

This essay is an effort to provide the spiritual seeker with some decidedly Jewish equipment for the journey to the Center that all wisdom-traditions embody in their essence. This equipment is not intended to be in any way comprehensive, but it should offer the sincere traveler some provisions on the path; if not manna from heaven, at least something to chew on while wandering through the desert. Some may be inspired to dig deeper into this rich storehouse of spiritual nourishment, thousands of years old, peopled with patriarchs and matriarchs, laden with legends, awash with commandments, saturated with faith in a Deity Whose ineffable Presence provides the holy glue holding it all together.

First, some clarification of the term *spirituality* is in order. I use the word to suggest that realm of experience that begins within us and connects us to the transcendent domain beyond us. It is not a term one can pin down with an exact definition. Certainly it encompasses soulfulness, which is to say imagination, creativity, intuition, the workings of the unconscious. It also includes a sense of unity-consciousness; that is, an awareness of the interconnectedness between all facets of existence—what Vietnamese monk Thich Nhat Hanh calls "interbeing." When I can experience myself in intimate relationship with a tree, a rock, an animal, or another human being and know that these are interrelated phenomena, that the boundary between myself and "other" is permeable, I am in a state of spiritual awareness. In this view, spirituality contains a "transrational" component—an intuitive leap to territory beyond where our merely rational faculties can guide us. Transrational territory is very different from irrational, in that it involves all our powers of discernment to reach the edge from which the flight takes place.

To explain what constitutes "Jewish" spirituality is to invoke the subjective realm of opinion: "Ask two Jews and you'll probably get three opinions." Is it the experience of God? Is it Jewish observance and ritual? Is it social justice—the emphasis on widows and orphans, the stranger, the homeless? My perspective on the matter is the basis of this essay. I have chosen three areas of focus to guide the reader along a Jewish path toward Truth, areas that in my opinion are central to the tradition, are broad enough to include several underlying themes, and are specifically related to practice. They each contain an experiential component that a dedicated seeker could use as a springboard into Jewish spiritual waters. (This desert path has a Sea of Reeds to traverse on the journey.) These three topics (reduced to one word each) are Torah, ritual, and covenant.

TORAH—THE JEWISH WINDOW OF ULTIMACY

The Torah is the central symbol of Judaism; it is the grappling hook that connects us to Ultimate Reality, also known as God. Or it could be viewed as the window through which we glimpse a transcendent dimension to our lives; the more transparent the window, the more the world becomes one with it. I have gathered these metaphors and many other seeds for ideas in this essay from the teachings of Ron Miller, one of the great spiritual teachers in my life. (See About the Authors at the end of this book.) In Jewish mystical terms, the Torah is believed to exist in heaven as white fire on black fire as well as inside the ark on earth (the ark being the curtained enclosure in a synagogue where the Torah resides). In this sacred text where human and divine elements coincide, religion has its aperture. The Torah (which means "divine teaching") could be regarded as the blueprint that God used to create the universe, or, more precisely, the Hebrew letters themselves that make up the Torah are also regarded by mystics as the building blocks of creation.

In concrete terms, the Torah consists of the first five books of the Hebrew Scriptures—Genesis, Exodus, Leviticus, Numbers, and Deuteronomy. Jewish tradition maintains that they were revealed to Moses on Mount Sinai about 1220 B.C.E., shortly after the Exodus from Egypt. Originally oral teachings, they did not reach their final written form until about 450 B.C.E. They contain a hearty mixture of narrative, legend, history, poetry, law, and mythology, covering events of the most cosmic significance (such as creation itself) down to the minutiae of day-to-day living (such as how to handle disputes over property). There is virtually nothing in our human experience and its relationship to the Divine that is not addressed in some way, shape, or form in the Torah. Sometimes one has to dig deep to find it, which is what students of Torah have been doing for almost 2,500 years. That it remains alive, vital, relevant and soul-nourishing is testimony to its genius, its artfulness, and its source in the wellsprings of eternal wisdom. To study this holy book is considered a form of prayer in Judaism. To embody it is to become one of the *tzadikim,* or righteous sages who somehow manage to live the message to such a degree that they are like living Torah scrolls.

Several interrelated themes come to mind in a discussion of Torah reading. One is the importance of interpretation, another is the crucial role of controversy, and a third is the centrality of speech and language in Judaism. I will elaborate on each of these, offering comments on their role in spiritual practice.

Interpretation: The Jewish Lens for Viewing the World

In Judaism, interpretation is vital to the text. It goes beyond being a legitimate activity; interpretation actually *becomes* the text. This is what occurred when the Talmud, which was originally oral law and commentary on the Torah, was written down (completed about 500 C.E.) and came to be considered a second Torah. Another huge body of interpretive work known as Midrash was completed several centuries earlier, and it too is an essential part of Torah study today. This vast branch of ancient rabbinic literature compiled by unknown authors consists of explanations, often in story form, that fill in the spaces between the words and lines of Scripture in order to make better sense out of them. The point of view may be devotional or ethical, words or passages may be clarified, laws may be explained. Midrash raises questions and attempts to answer them. The explanations become as important as the lines of text themselves. To quote the great twentieth-century Jewish philosopher Franz Rosenzweig: "God came down on Sinai. That is revelation. The rest is interpretation."

I find this emphasis on interpretation very satisfying, because it allows for an interplay between text and interpreter that includes imagination and creativity. The very subjectivity of the interpretation gives it existential depth and a certain soulfulness. Midrash lives and breathes; it is the reverse of being written in stone.

Interpretation also allows the tradition to evolve, so that laws and ethical mandates can be understood in relation to our current concerns. While the final legal code in Judaism was written in the sixteenth century C.E. (the *Shulkhan Arukh*, or dinner-table of law where one is invited to partake of ultimate nourishment), new questions continue to be raised and grappled with as new social, political, and psychological issues are confronted. These questions and answers are written in the *responsa* literature, an ongoing system of Jewish interpretation by major rabbinic minds today. Clearly, to remain vital, any tradition must speak to the issues of the day: questions regarding AIDS, homosexuality, abortion, racial discrimination, women's rights (to name a few) must be sifted through the centuries of related wisdom and addressed with the immediacy of the moment.

Here are a few examples of midrash, just to offer a flavor of it.

It is said that God spoke to each of the Israelites at Sinai in the voice that he or she could best understand. So at the moment of revelation, the timid souls heard a gentle voice, the intrepid heard a thunderous voice, the romantics heard a melodious voice, each according to her need. This speaks to me of the uniqueness that the experience of God offers, no two experiences being identical. It also addresses the inadequacy of language to describe, in any kind of universal way, the ineffable. One meets the Divine in the context of a particular, subjective "I-Thou" encounter, to use the wonderful terminology of Martin Buber, the twentieth-century existentialist.

Another midrash states that Moses heard not only the entire written Torah on Sinai but the entire oral Torah as well, including every question raised to the end of history. This has profound philosophical implications. Unlike the Greek mind, which revises by getting rid of the old, the Hebrew mind does not throw anything out. One is fortunate just to get the questions; there is no such thing as *the* answer. This view has the ring of truth for me.

A third midrash (going back in time, but chronological sequence is said not to be relevant in Torah, whose frame of reference is eternal) comments that Jacob's descent into Egypt was Israel's first diaspora, believed to be part of God's plan. The Rabbis picture Jacob struggling over the decision whether to remain in Canaan or settle in Egypt, but finally deciding to leave because God willed him to go. Here the interplay between human and divine, between free will and heavenly intercession becomes paramount. That God deliberately sends the Israelites into Egypt, and oppression speaks to the paradox of the relationship between God and

Israel. God loves His people yet sets the stage for their tremendous suffering as slaves. Slavery appears to be a necessary ingredient for the emergence of the Jewish people as a community of free, self-willed individuals capable of entering into the covenant with God. And in a related midrash, God goes into exile too and weeps with the people in their suffering.

What are the implications of all this with regard to spiritual practice? As I see it, one is given permission to establish a living dialogue with Scripture, using it as a jumping off point for one's own midrash, based on one's own understanding. This affords the opportunity to look deeply into the text and see beyond the literal into the philosophical, the metaphorical, and the transcendent realms.

The following exercise may illustrate the point. Open the Torah to virtually any page and choose a passage to read slowly, carefully, with an attitude of receptivity. Breathe mindfully for a minute or two before attempting the reading, however—that is, with attention to each breath, as a way of clearing the mental palate. Then read the selected verse several times with great attention to detail. See what comes to you in relation to the passage. Just as in dream interpretation, open the door to whatever thoughts, memories, or associations occur to you. I mention dreams quite specifically, as I have found the language of the unconscious to be particularly conducive for exploring God-territory.

In attempting this exercise myself, I opened to Exodus 22:30: "You shall be men holy to Me: you must not eat flesh torn by beasts in the field; you shall cast it to the dogs." This is not a passage that I have studied before, nor has it had any particular meaning to me in the past. I find the patriarchal language unsettling, as always. I remind myself of the times and circumstances in which this was written, transcend the narrowness, and substitute "people" for "men." I wonder why the translation *is* "men" here, when *anshei-kodesh* could also be translated "holy people" (literally, "people of holiness"), and make a mental note to check other translations. I recall similar biblical statements, as when we are told, "You shall be to Me . . . a holy nation" (Exodus 19:6), and later in Leviticus 19:2, "You shall be holy, for I, the Lord your God am holy" (which I will discuss later). I think about what it means to be "holy" to God. It is a word that implies separation, a division between the sacred and the profane. I reflect on this division and wonder about it. Isn't the issue really to seek the sacred *within* the profane; to find the spark of divinity that exists in all things? I think of a poem that I wrote once on this subject, implying that sacred and profane were one. Yet I recognize that some boundaries are necessary to create order out of chaos. The next line about not eating flesh torn by beasts stirs up many associations—the whole notion of being mindful of what we eat, that how we nourish ourselves has spiritual meaning, the elaborate laws of *kashrut* (dietary restrictions) that come later in the Torah, my decision a year ago to become a vegetarian. Then I think about my dog, to whom I would not wish to cast torn flesh. Yet as spiritual a being as he is, in my estimation (in his simplicity, honesty, and "creatureliness"), I appreciate the separation that divides us, which is one of mindfulness, or awareness. Now I might come up with a midrash about holiness involving food consumption: Perhaps that which separates us from lower animals is our conscious wish to be close to God, which entails some self-restraint in what we eat. I could go on and create a fanciful tale about my dog if I wished.

Obviously, each person would have a different set of responses to this material. A year ago, my reaction would have been different. (I didn't have a dog and I wasn't a vegetarian.) A year from now, it may go off in a totally divergent direction, raising new questions and prompting unforeseen associations. The point is that our lives play on Scripture in creative ways, inspiring us to ask questions and to search for meaning that has relevance both eternally and *now*. It was said by Franz Rosenzweig, a Jewish philosopher early in this century, that our lives are like a spotlight, illuminating the text. The Jewish tradition is one of endless dialogue with this God-given, human-interpreted material. The same page of Talmud is discussed every day around the world. The same weekly Torah portion (known as the *parasha*) is discussed cyclically throughout the year (so that the entire Torah is read once in a year) wherever Jews congregate. The premise is that the teachings are unlimited in scope; new insights will be gained because of our continuing growth, which opens us up to new possibilities with each reading. The Talmud begins on page two, just as the Torah begins with the second letter of the Hebrew alphabet, *bet*, rather than the first letter, *aleph*. They are beginning-less and endless, like the teachings themselves.

Wrestling with the Angel: The Importance of Controversy in Jewish Thought

Related to interpretation is the notion of controversy. Most questions have multiple answers, often contradictory answers, which collectively point to the truth. The truth we can arrive at, then, is an approximation that shines through the struggle with polarities; it is an ambiguous rather than a solid entity. That is as close as one can get to an Absolute. In Jewish tradition, asking the right question may be considered more valuable than coming up with the right answer.

The Rabbinic Bible (*Mikra'ot G'dolot*) is a graphic illustration of how diversity of opinion is central to Jewish thinking. On each page is a small portion of Torah text surrounded by commentary (including the Aramaic translation, which is a commentary of its own). These medieval commentators (all male, unfortunately, but such were the times) present an amazing array of often conflicting ideas as to the meaning of the text. Thus, a serious student of Torah studies the text in the company of minds like the amazing Rashi (an eleventh-century French scholar whose grasp of Scripture is legendary), Maimonides (the brilliant twelfth-century rationalist philosopher whose landmark treatise *Guide to the Perplexed* is the inspiration for this essay's title), Nachmanides (the extraordinary thirteenth-century mystic), and a host of learned others. These gentlemen seldom agree with one another, and the resulting mixture of opinions is juicy. Add to this broth your own mind and, if possible, that of your colleagues (study, as opposed to reading, must take place with at least one other person in Jewish tradition), and you have quite a bowl of bouillabaisse (which may not be kosher but is very tasty). Thus, the Rabbinic Bible suggests the complexity, depth, and infinite possibilities inherent in Scripture.

I also find it intriguing that unanimity is mistrusted in Jewish thought. In the Sanhedrin (the Jewish high courts of ancient Judea), if a guilty verdict was unanimous, the suspect would be let go (or in a capital case, not executed). A unanimous verdict would arouse suspicions of bribery, or the assumption that no judge had actively sought exonerating evidence. Again, differing sides are viewed as essential to arrive at the truth.

Thus controversy, like interpretation, is central to the nature of language, words, and our understanding of them, since the words we choose are always a matter of perspective. Every interpretation is partial, provisional, and imperfect. This is part of the human predicament, but also part of the beauty and preciousness of being human. It underscores our precariousness, our vulnerability. Our imperfect approximations are nonetheless authentic encounters; they are wrestlings with the angel that help to transform us, just as Jacob was transformed into Israel (which means "one who struggles with God") in Genesis 32:25–29. Judaism rightly celebrates the effort to arrive at truth through impassioned disagreement and dialogue.

How does controversy relate to spiritual practice? I believe that it affords the honest seeker the opportunity to respectfully disagree. It allows more space for one's own opinion, however divergent that opinion might be from the prevailing view. And it suggests that wrestling with alternate points of view has value in determining where one stands on an issue.

A personal anecdote may illustrate the point, but first, some background information to help clarify it. My desire to become steeped in one wisdom tradition stems from a mind-set that is passionately pluralistic. Personal encounters with both Christianity and Buddhism preceded my entrance into the rabbinical seminary, where I am currently a student, and have been vital to my spiritual growth. I devoutly believe that, like the spokes of a wheel, many paths lead to the same Center, each with its unique contribution and particular strength. This diversity of vehicles to the Center feels as necessary to me as the many names of God in the Torah. The unfolding of relationships with the Absolute into a multicolored tapestry of limitless designs speaks to the richness and complexity of spiritual endeavor.

Thus, in one of my classes (during a discussion of what constitutes idol worship), I mentioned that I have a small statue of the Buddha on the altar before which I meditate and pray at home. He sits in the lotus position in front of a large piece of cardboard displaying the tetragrammaton (the four Hebrew letters *yod hey vav hey* designating the holiest, unpronounceable name of God). Next to the Buddha is a candle, which helps illuminate the bold, black letters. The inclusion of this statue in my place of prayer excited considerable controversy among the group. Was I violating the commandment forbidding worship of graven images? Could I rightly call myself a Jew with such behavior, let alone a would-be rabbi? I explained that for me, the Buddha is a symbol of a body of teachings that have brought me closer to Ultimate Reality. For that, I am grateful to Buddhism and therefore enjoy having this symbol on my altar; it helps me to create a sacred space and to feel nearer to God. In no way do I worship the Buddha or bow down to him. (Neither do most Buddhists, I might add.) I don't confuse the Buddha with God, nor do I confuse the name of God on the piece of cardboard with God. The statue represents a wise teacher of Dharma, the Buddhist teachings; the tetragrammaton represents the holiest name in Torah, the Jewish teachings. Both are symbols enabling me to feel closer to the ineffable Presence. Both come from the same Source and are "very good."

The ensuing discussion occurred because I could feel safe enough to openly express my ideas in a tradition that values difference of opinion—having the Buddha on my *bima* would not excommunicate me, even if it was initially regarded with surprise and suspicion. Disagreement is viewed as a necessary aspect of dialogue that leads to a fuller understanding of the subject under consideration. The object is not necessarily consensus (as the Rabbinic Bible demonstrates, with its conflicting commentaries side by side); the object is to respectfully examine all points of view. Our human understanding must learn to accommodate diversity of thoughts and ambiguity in defining right and wrong. When no consensus can be arrived at, both opinions are left intact, and Jewish tradition says when the *Mashiakh* (Messiah) arrives, the issue will be decided.

The Importance of Speech and Language, Words and Names, in Judaism

"Open my mouth, O Lord, and my lips will proclaim Your praise"—these words begin the Amidah, the central prayer in the Jewish service, traditionally recited three times a day. The capacity to speak is not taken lightly in Judaism. Indeed, God is depicted as creating the world with ten Sayings (beginning "God said") in the first chapter of Genesis. In Jewish mysticism, the term "circumcision of the tongue" denotes fluency in Hebrew and Torah and an ability to probe and utilize their mysteries. This fluency is connected to the covenantal relationship with God (which will be discussed later).

Thus, in the Book of Exodus, Moses had to have his tongue circumcised (metaphorically) in order to speak to Pharaoh and in order to speak to the Israelites such that they would listen to him. Interestingly, he was not a natural orator, but was said to be "slow of speech and heavy of tongue." (There is a midrash about him burning his tongue as a baby and being left with a speech impediment.) It is ironic that in a tradition that so values words, one of our greatest heroes was not initially a man of words at all. Instead, Moses was a man who acted on impulse, for example, striking the rock to draw water from it, rather than using the appropriate word. (And, for this, he was said to be denied entrance to the Promised Land.) Previously he acted out of anger by killing the Egyptian who was beating a Hebrew and by smashing the first set of tablets containing the Ten Commandments (which, according to the Talmud, had already lost their words, in response to the idolatry that had occurred). When God instructs Moses to carve the words himself on the second set of tablets, he is given an essential lesson about the power and value of words. Perhaps this is a lesson we each need to learn, both as individuals and as members of a spiritual community.

Finding one's authentic voice as Moses ultimately did is an issue that speaks vibrantly to me. Only in the last four or five years have I discovered what feels to be my authentic voice through poetry and spirituality, after a long, dry period of desert wandering and struggle. To find our truest voice is to touch something deep within ourselves, that space where a reservoir of ardor and intensity resides and can emerge. This space is the source of *kavannah*—a Jewish mystical term that suggests the profound inwardness, concentration, and devotion necessary both for prayer and for becoming who we really are. To connect to this space, then, has implications for spiritual practice. To relate to something with kavannah is to find the right words for it; that is, words that express our own truths, that help define our own experience. Such words can be enormously empowering, because they enable us to better understand how we feel and who we are. They allow us to know ourselves more deeply. Writing a poem actually reinterprets the world for me. I find that poetry comes closer than ordinary language. As an illustration, I share the following poem entitled "*Sheckinah,*" which means "She Who Dwells with Us":

> *God is manifest everywhere—*
> *in the air I breathe,*
> *in the thoughts I think,*
> *in the tears I shed.*
> *Immanent and transcendent*
> *She hears me, speaks through me, answers me.*
> *She dwells in the vast spaces between my atoms*
> *where particles travel like rockets on a sacred mission.*
> *I am saturated with Her.*

Gratefully gracefully
I gather Her light
and She finds solace in me.
She wrote this poem with me.

In his luminous book *In Speech and in Silence,* David Wolpe writes movingly about the Jewish legacy of language. He also touches on the paradox of silence. He depicts the horror of being trapped in a silent world (after his mother's stroke, she is unable to use language meaningfully), and the wonder of silence, which moves beyond the expressible to the realm of the ineffable. When God says, "Be still and know Me," She speaks to the truth that lies beyond language. While speech remains central to Jewish tradition, it is nonetheless inadequate. It directs us to the reality, but is not Ultimate Reality, which can never be named. Speech and language are a way of approaching the mystery that transcends them.

In Jewish thinking, names are a means of deeply knowing someone, perhaps having power over someone via the name (or more accurately, via the knowing). In a midrash, the biblical Adam is given the opportunity to name both himself and God, as a way of establishing greater intimacy. In the Book of Exodus, after being told that he is to be the spokesperson for the Israelites, Moses asks God for His name, so that he can inform the people of exactly who sent him. God answers mysteriously, *"Ehyeh Asher Ehyeh"*—a magnificently ambiguous answer that suggests both the present and future tenses of the verb *to be.* Thus, God might be saying "I am what I am," or "I am what I will be," or "I will be what I am," or even "what will be will be."

The holiest name of God, the aforementioned tetragrammaton, is both unpronounceable and unknowable. It was pronounced in the days of the Temple, but only on Yom Kippur (the Day of Atonement) by the High Priest in the Holy of Holies (the innermost sanctum where the ark was kept). For the last two thousand years, since the destruction of the Temple, it has not been pronounced by anyone. The tetragrammaton is referred to as *Shem ham'forash,* or the ineffable name. Paradoxically, the literal translation of the phrase is "the name clearly interpreted and expressed." The Hebrew phrase thus contains both aspects of the mystery—that God is ineffable and that God must be continually interpreted, explained, clarified. This speaks to the notion that the Absolute can never be fully articulated; to attempt to do so is a form of idolatry. Judaism is a tradition of hope and humility. It recognizes that we can approach the mystery but reminds us that our human limitations prevent us from knowing it fully.

Meditating on the different names of God is a spiritual practice central to Jewish mysticism. (There are seventy names of God in the Torah.) For the practitioner with a mystical bent, I suggest the following exercises, similar to some of the practices in Aryeh Kaplan's fascinating book called *Jewish Meditation*. Write the four Hebrew letters of the tetragrammaton on a piece of cardboard. You needn't have any prior understanding of Hebrew to do this; simply copy them from a Torah or prayer book. Now sit quietly with them, breathing them in and allowing them to occupy your mind, as a sort of visual mantra. You can pronounce each letter separately, as your eyes move from letter to letter: *yod hey vav hey*. Become very comfortable in their presence; let them feel familiar to you. This may take several or many sittings, and may be as far as you wish to go. It is a powerful practice unto itself. If you wish to go further, let your imagination open to touch their spiritual energy. Picture the letters as large as buildings, perhaps palaces. Enter each one and walk through its rooms. Surround yourself in them. Use whatever images come to you spontaneously and creatively but stay focused on the letters. Be aware of your response to the exercise but have no preconceived notions of what that response should be. You are training yourself to feel the Presence of God, an experience with as many individual variations as there are individuals.

JEWISH RITUAL—A WAY TO THE CENTER

Ritual is the enactment of a tradition's basic symbols (the connecting links to Ultimacy) and myths (the symbols in narrative form) by a community of practitioners. I am using definitions drawn from the wisdom of Ron Miller. The purpose of ritual is to allow the external structure to bring us closer to the internal workings of Ultimate Reality. Put another way, it is to enable us to be more God-centered in our daily lives. Rituals are reminders of who we are and where we come from. If used to their fullest capacity, they can steer us on our path to deeper encounters with what makes life worth living: realms of mystery that include love, faith, awe, and interconnectedness.

Jewish tradition is laden with rituals. Some involve rites of passage, such as circumcision (eight days after birth), *bar mitzvahs* and *bat mitzvahs* (to celebrate a child's readiness to take on more adult responsibilities in the community; literally to become sons and daughters of the commandments), weddings, and funerals. Others are connected to the festival days sprinkled throughout the Jewish calendar, from *Rosh Hashanah* (the Jewish New Year), to *Tisha b'Av* (a day of mourning commemorating the destruction of the ancient Temples). The weekly Sabbath practices of *Shabbat* are a jewel in the crown of Judaism. Daily prayer involving the use of *tallit* (prayer shawl) and *tefillin* (phylacteries bound by leather straps to the forehead and arm) constitutes another form of ritual for the very observant Jew. Laws of *kashrut* (dietary restrictions) are another major area of daily ritual. The degree of observance ranges from the secular Jew, who might be married and buried by a rabbi but finds little else of value in ritual, to the Orthodox Jew, who is steeped in it from morning to night.

My upbringing was in a secular Jewish household where religious observance was minimal to nonexistent. We never lit Sabbath candles, observed any of the dietary laws, or said prayers and blessings. Shabbat was not set apart as a special day, remembered and kept holy. God was not mentioned, except as an expletive. We did belong to a Reform congregation, but like many other families in our neighborhood, we attended services only on what are known as the "High Holidays" of Rosh Hashanah and Yom Kippur (the Day of Atonement and the holiest day of the year). We neither fasted on Yom Kippur nor refrained from eating leavened bread on Passover.

Occasionally we attended a Passover seder (the ritual retelling of the Exodus story, which forms the central narrative of Judaism) with extended-family members, but never held the celebration in our own home. We did observe the religiously less significant holiday of Chanukah, lighting the candelabra known as a *menorah* and exchanging gifts over the eight-day period. I think this had to do with the festival's proximity to Christmas and a need to take part in the wider culture's sense of celebration. There was an unspoken attitude of discomfort and perhaps some contempt toward ritualistic expression of religious devotion as unsophisticated and phony.

Thus my personal relationship with Jewish ritual contains a mixture of sometimes conflicting feelings. While I have no difficulty appreciating the value of symbolic reenactments (such as the Passover seder, which enacts the exodus of the Jews from Egypt, or the observance of the Sabbath, which enacts God's original ordering of the world at creation), I still feel an awkwardness in publicly reciting blessings. I am much more "at home" talking to God in the privacy of my study, using my own words, gestures, chants, and songs. However, I am enthusiastic about experiencing the power of communal prayer and wish to learn more about this vital aspect of Jewish tradition. The whole area of finding meaning in ritual is very much in process in my life. It is a rich realm that all spiritual seekers should be advised to explore.

Neil Gilman has a thought-provoking chapter on ritual in his excellent book *Sacred Fragments*. He raises the question of why we need ritual in our lives at all, and comes up with some intriguing answers. He speaks of the structuring role of a community's myths through ritual expressions. Myth, a most misunderstood term, refers in this context to the deepest, truest communal explanations for the meaning of human experience, expressed poetically rather than factually, since metaphor is the only way to approach the transcendent dimension. So ritual becomes, in part, an answer to the intuitive human need to create order out of chaos by structuring reality. A *mezuzah* (a small container with passages from Torah on parchment) is placed on the doorpost of one's home to separate public from private and to designate respect for God's laws. Some people kiss it before leaving their homes. Rituals distinguishing thresholds in time are even more prevalent: Jews recite liturgies upon waking up, going to sleep, marking the Sabbath's coming and going, marking the beginning of each month and the new year. Finally, as Gilman eloquently states, "the great moments in the Jewish year and in a Jewish life are sanctified by elaborate pageants where liturgy and ritual—the language of words and the language of the body—come together, each doing what it does best." From circumcision to seder to *Kaddish* (the prayer for the dead), rituals organize and enrich Jewish lives, imbuing them with shared meaning. By bringing the depth of myth into our tangible experience, rituals enable a community to bond and to establish living traditions that can be transmitted over generations. A sense of identity is created that gives body and form to the intangible and unnamable realities.

Gilman also raises the important question, "Isn't it enough to be a good person?" Clearly, being a good person is what Judaism is all about. Ultimately, ritual's sole purpose is to facilitate the kind of God-centered behavior that enables us to be good people. It is never an end in itself, to be worshipped and revered as an Absolute. If ritual is doing its job, it is an impetus to moral behavior that leads to increased compassion, concern for the oppressed, and love of oneself and one's companions on the planet. If this is not the result, then the ritual needs to be examined, modified, or discarded.

With that said, I would like to discuss three aspects of Jewish ritual that illustrate the process of becoming God-centered. One relates to Yom Kippur and the role of atonement in dealing with the mystery of evil. A second topic involves the centrality of the seder in Jewish life and its relationship to freedom. A third section will look more globally at how spirituality permeates everyday life in Judaism through its use of ritual. Each of these topics will provide ideas for the spiritual practitioner to chew on and try out, if the taste is appealing.

Judaism placess less emphasis on sin, evil, and "the fall" than does Christianity, and perhaps more emphasis on a forgiving God. Rather than talking so much about sin, Jews speak of how we inevitably "miss the mark" as part of our human nature, and therefore we need forgiveness. Thus the importance of Yom Kippur—the Day of Atonement—in the cycle of Jewish holidays. This holiest day of the year, known as the Sabbath of Sabbaths, is preceded by ten days of individual and collective soul-searching known as the Days of Awe during which *teshuvah*—"repentance" but, more literally, "returning"—takes place. The returning is to one's original ethical and spiritual nature, one's innate goodness. This restores a sense of wholeness or *shalom* to the individual.

As Estelle Frankel points out in a recent article in *Tikkun* magazine (in one of the finest accounts of how spiritual and psychological healing occur), atonement provides "at-one-ment" with God, with one another, and with our own selves. These Days of Awe allow us to review our mistakes of the past year, to accept responsibility for them, to reset our moral compass, to let go of guilt, and to start the new year with renewed purpose and a clean slate. On Yom Kippur, judgment gives way to compassion and forgiveness—an awesome transformation, indeed.

It is noteworthy that the first Yom Kippur took place in the desert, when Moses descended Mount Sinai with the second set of tablets, having smashed the first (those sacred, meaningful fragments) in a fit of rage over the Israelites' worshipping a golden calf. The second set of tablets (containing the Ten Commandments) were a sign that God had forgiven the Jewish people (and Moses for his destructive anger) because they had repented. Aaron, who had participated in creating the golden calf, is appointed High Priest—he is a repentant sinner and thus can be raised up. The energy of sin can be transformed into actual merit through teshuvah. In fact, the Talmud says that a higher status is granted to a repentant sinner (*ba'al teshuvah*, or "master of returning") than to the righteous saint who never strayed from the path—an encouraging state of affairs for most of us.

The steps to *teshuvah* that Maimonides outlines are useful to consider. First there is awareness, that is, mindfulness of wrongdoing. Next is verbal confession of the sin, followed by an expression of regret, which is necessary to learn the deepest lessons from our mistakes (and, which Frankel points out, also requires self-forgiveness and acceptance). Finally comes the resolution not to repeat the sin again. Offering restitution when possible to those we have harmed by our wrongdoing is a fifth step. Repentance is complete when we encounter a similar situation (as, inevitably, we will) and manage to do it differently. I am struck by how relevant this medieval philosopher's understanding is to our postmodern world. The more things change, the more they stay the same.

I am also impressed with Frankel's notion that teshuvah contains "a kind of time travel" in it, allowing us to access the past and the future through God (the tetragrammaton having within it the sense of was, is, and will be; that is, standing outside of time). This brings me back to a retreat with Vietnamese Buddhist monk Thich Nhat Hanh in 1993, his gentle, powerful voice explaining that when you touch the present moment deeply, you can also touch the past, and even change it, that is, heal it. Similarly, when you live the present moment deeply, you can touch the future, that is, care for it. He said, "The light of mindfulness is the energy of God" (an uncharacteristic mention of God for a Buddhist). It is this energy that makes the transformation, which is really a unification, possible. The *yaetzer ha-ra* (evil inclination) and *yaetzer ha-tov* (good inclination) both contain the *yaetzer*, or energy source. The idea is not to get rid of our inclinations but to transform them through at-one-ment.

Central to Jewish understanding, then, is the belief that we are not intrinsically evil or corrupt. We contain within us a seed that is the image of God, our basic goodness. We are given the gift of free will and the curse of the yaetzer ha-ra, but we are also given the opportunity for transformation and the blessing of God's forgiveness when we do miss the mark. What's more, we are given a guidebook on the path, which is our best means of avoiding sin. That guidebook, as previously mentioned, is the primary symbol linking us to the Divine. It is the Jewish form of grace. It is the Torah. Our most effective resource for avoiding sin is the Source: By following the teachings and doing the *mitzvot* (or commandments), our path is lit. Even so, we are likely to stumble and perhaps fall. The traditional Christian question, "Are you saved?" is simply not a Jewish question. It would be better worded "Are you forgiven?" The answer is, if your teshuvah has kavannah, of course you are forgiven.

The implications for spiritual practice are profound. Each of us knows the disquietude of wrongdoing and the need to regain one's balance in the face of it. Spend some contemplative time sorting through your actions of the recent past. Choose a particular instance where you missed the mark. Bring as much of it into awareness as possible, recalling the details as completely and vividly as you can. Think of exactly who was harmed by your action and what the consequences were. Allow yourself to feel genuine regret, taking responsibility for your part in it without flagellating yourself. This is a delicate balance, because self-acceptance must accompany the process if it is to be effective. Harshness and excessive guilt actually get in the way of forgiveness. Express in words both the wrongdoing and the regret, either aloud or in writing. Articulating this is important, as the words are powerful containers and will aid in the ultimate transformation. Share the incident with a trusted friend, teacher, or spiritual advisor. If this feels impossible, share it aloud to God. Preferably, do both. Resolve not to make this error again, and ask God for help in the resolution. Be very open to whatever support suggests itself at this point in the process, as help may be provided in unexpected ways. Next, make whatever restitution is possible to the person or persons who were harmed. This could range from heartfelt apology to actual material compensation. If they cannot be contacted physically, then do so with your thoughts, touching the past by living very intensely and authentically in the present moment. Know that even if the individuals involved cannot forgive you, God can and will forgive you. When the opportunity to commit a similar offense occurs and you succeed in your effort not to repeat it, then teshuvah is complete. *Mazel tov* (congratulations)!

The Passover *Seder*–The Journey from Slavery to Liberation

The Exodus story—the grand saga of slavery in Egypt, Moses' confrontation with Pharaoh, the plagues, the escape, the parting of the sea, the culmination in revelation at Sinai—is the central narrative of Jewish tradition. It is retold in the Haggadah (which means "the telling"), a small book that for the past five hundred years has become the most widely reprinted text in Judaism, with close to three thousand editions. Every denomination and subgroup has come up with its own distinctive retelling of the story, with subtle differences in emphasis and varying commentaries. I have drawn inspiration from Rabbi Rami Shapiro's poetic rendering of the ritual, which served my family well during Passover of 1995. Reading the Haggadah aloud is a response to the Torah's command to teach one's children the story; few other mitzvot are as widely observed as this one. On this Jewish holiday, even the most secular of Jews are drawn together to celebrate liberation from slavery and the birth of a people in the ritual event par excellence of the year.

The story is central to the Book of Exodus in the Torah. The Jews who were initially welcomed into Egypt are now confronted by a cruel Pharaoh "who did not know Joseph" (Exodus 1:8; Joseph being the Hebrew slave who became Pharaoh's right-hand man in a prior generation) and who enslaves and oppresses them ruthlessly. Frightened of their potential power, the Egyptian king attempts to murder all male infants born to the Jews. Hidden in a floating ark on the Nile, the baby Moses escapes this fate and is rescued and brought up by Pharaoh's daughter as a prince of Egypt. Enraged by the harsh treatment he witnesses, Moses kills an Egyptian overseer who was beating a Hebrew and is forced to flee Egypt to Midian. There he tends sheep, marries Zipporah, and encounters God in a burning bush in the wilderness.

Moses has been chosen to lead the Jews to freedom, which he does valiantly, if reluctantly. With the help of his brother Aaron and sister Miriam, he manages to raise the consciousness of the people, planting the seeds of rebellion and the desire for freedom. All the negotiations with the unyielding Pharaoh are doomed to failure, even with God inflicting plagues of increasing intensity on the people, until the tenth plague resulting in the death of the firstborn children of Egypt. On this night (the fourteenth of *Nisan*, the night of the first seder), the Israelites are instructed to smear a bit of lamb's blood on the doorposts of their homes so that the Angel of Death would pass over (*pesach*, in Hebrew) their houses and spare their children. The lamb, it should be noted, was an Egyptian deity, and its slaughter therefore symbolized rebellion against idolatry. Stricken with grief and fear, Pharaoh allows the Jews a hasty exit, taking with them the unleavened bread known as *matzah*, since the dough they had prepared did not have time to rise. However, his anger is soon rekindled, and he chases the Jews to the Sea of Reeds (often translated Red Sea), which is miraculously split, allowing the Jews to escape over dry land but drowning the Egyptian army. This physical liberation sets the stage for the spiritual birth that is to occur at Sinai with God's revelation.

A wonderful midrash teaches that at the drowning of the Egyptians, when the Israelites broke into wild song and celebration, God's voice rebuked them, thundering from the heavens: "You dare rejoice at the death of my children? There is no joy in death. The cost of freedom is most awesome; respect it always!" With compassion for human suffering, then, Jews mark the plagues by removing from their wine cups a drop of wine for each plague, so as not to take pleasure in another's pain.

As this example indicates, what makes Passover so powerful is that the retelling of the story is accompanied by a variety of actions to reinforce its messages. In observant households, the ritual activity starts well ahead of the seder, in that the Jewish home must be cleansed of *chametz*, or leaven. It is regarded as a symbol of the yaetzer ha-ra; one needs liberation from its corrupting influence. Here we witness the interdependence in Judaism of ritual and ethics. A thorough spring cleaning is the tradition, culminating in a ceremony where, by candlelight, parents and children remove the final crumbs of bread (strategically placed) from corners and windowsills with a feather. The following morning, they are burned.

At the seder (which means "order" in the sense of agenda or procedure), participants are instructed to recline in their chairs rather than sit upright (sometimes pillows are provided) to signify a people at rest in freedom. A seder plate is arranged with a wide spectrum of symbolic foods, some of which are eaten in the course of the evening. Matzah is provided to symbolize the bread of affliction and the notion that eating a poor man's food in freedom is preferable to eating well in slavery. Also, it represents our solidarity with the oppressed and our commitment to freeing those who suffer from injustice. A roasted shankbone represents the paschal lamb (vegetarians can substitute a broiled beet); a green vegetable symbolizes the rebirth of spring; *haroset* (a mixture of nuts, apples, spices, and wine) is the mortar the Hebrew slaves produced for their Egyptian masters; *maror* (bitter herbs, often horseradish) marks the bitterness of bondage and oppression. Four cups of wine are drunk at various points of the ceremony, and a fifth cup is filled for the prophet Elijah (the prophet who will one day announce the arrival of the Messiah), who is said to visit every seder and drink a few drops. Near the end of the ceremony, the door is opened for him.

For all its emphasis on oppression, which begins with our ancestors' outcry of despair, the essence of the evening is a joyous celebration of liberty. Children are very deliberately drawn into the festivities, asking the ritual questions (most notably, "Why is this

night different from all other nights?") and participating in the
singing, the discussing, the dipping (into bitter herbs, into salt
water), the retelling. They are involved to the very end of the seder,
searching for the *afikoman* (the hidden piece of matzah symbolizing
the mystery of things, how more of life is hidden than is revealed),
which serves as dessert and concludes the meal. Everyone is
instructed to remember that once we were slaves in Egypt but that
God delivered us "with a mighty hand and an outstretched arm"
(Deuteronomy 6:21). This is a reminder that occurs regularly in
Jewish prayers, to make us ever cognizant of the gift of freedom, of
God's role in providing it, of our responsibility in maintaining it
and striving for the freedom of all people everywhere. Another
theme central to Passover is gratitude, best expressed in the song
"*Dayyenu,*" which means "it would have been sufficient." This
refrain is sung repeatedly, as each miracle and each kindness that
God provided Israel is recounted and regarded as sufficient by
itself. Thus liberty, solidarity, faith, and gratitude all unite on this
ritual occasion of remembrance and joy.

The Hebrew word for Egypt is *Mitzraim,* which also signifies
the narrow places, the tight spots that grip us. From the point of
view of spiritual practice, Passover entreats us to examine our own
ongoing struggle for liberation from the narrow places in our lives,
the rigidities in our thinking. As Arthur Waskow (of the Alliance
for Jewish Renewal) puts it, we are enjoined to face the Pharaohs of
the present time, using the past as inspiration to deal with our own
outcries of despair. The ancient event must be relived precisely
because it is so pertinent to present tyrannies, whether political,
economic, psychological, or spiritual. Waskow suggests that everyone seated around the seder table pledge to do one act of facing
Pharaoh, such as calling a radio talk show or a member of Congress
to express a view consistent with freedom and compassion. To this,
I would add facing our internal Pharaohs—the fears that can hold
us prisoner within our families, workplaces, friendships. Examine a
tight spot that has you immobilized and shine the light of mindfulness on it. Make some effort toward softening it, loosening its hold

on you, and see what can be born from the fearful narrows, passing through the sea of awareness and out into the spacious wilderness where the Source is surely present. *Dayyenu!*

Spirituality Permeates Everyday Life

Spirituality is not separate from our day-to-day life experience in Judaism. As the Jewish existentialist philosopher Martin Buber said, "The world is not an obstacle on the way; it *is* the way." We are encouraged toward a mind-set of "blessed participation" in the world (Ron Miller's term), by becoming conscious of the sacred character of everyday life. One way of achieving this is to say actual blessings throughout the day. Judaism has available what must be the largest compendium of blessings for every imaginable experience: One can say blessings upon waking up, going to sleep, eating, drinking (with variations relating to what one eats or drinks, be it wine, bread, pastry, fruits, vegetables), going to the bathroom (we acknowledge the gift of our body with its amazing plumbing system), meeting a friend after a long absence, studying Torah, seeing lightning, hearing thunder, gazing at the ocean, noticing a flowering tree, admiring a rainbow. On a recent flight from New Orleans to Chicago, I encountered an Israeli named Shmuel who had a book-length blessing to be said before taking off in an airplane. All of this is to emphasize that the deeper dimension exists right here in this world, which is fully invested with the sacredness of the Divine.

Each blessing has both a transcendent reference ("Praised are You *Adonai* our God") and a reference to the material realm ("Who brings forth bread from the earth"). In the Hebrew tradition, body and soul are not fundamentally separate. A person is viewed as having dimensions but also as being one integral being whose essence is a unity of flesh, soul, and spirit. Thus sexuality is considered holy, and sexual union between man and wife on Shabbat is a mitzvah—a good deed that contributes to the unification of God. (More about that in the next section.) One's connection to spirit does not erase the body and soul; it enhances them. Jews are challenged to sanctify all of life. Rather than experiencing the world as divided into categories of sacred and profane, we are encouraged to sacralize the profane by perceiving its divine dimension. In this way, spirit infuses every aspect of living.

This is not to say that Judaism has no notion of abstinence in its laws. Certainly there are strict regulations involving sexual conduct, eating (the laws of kashrut), fast days, the Sabbath. Blessed participation in life does not mean unlimited or unregulated participation. But the regulations imposed are very different from the "holy abstinence" model of early Christianity where the body and physical world had to be negated in order to achieve a spiritual consciousness. Judaism insists that the material world is not intrinsically evil and the pleasures of life are to be discerned and enjoyed.

The Talmud even states that on the day of judgment, you will be called to account for all the beauties of the world in which you failed to participate. As Alice Walker's character Shug, in *The Color Purple*, so memorably puts it: "I think it pisses God off if you walk by the color purple in a field somewhere and don't notice it." We are called to notice, to pay attention, to look deeply.

The result of such perception is the discovery of our own divinity. Within each of us is the divine spark that reflects the image of God. Knowledge of this spark is experiential, not intellectual, and usually comes only after considerable journeying on the path. The Jewish experiential philosopher Abraham Joshua Heschel describes a mind-set of "giving glory" in relation to ourselves and the universe. We recognize awe within ourselves, that sense of wonder at the marvels of creation that leads to a birth of glory. Then we recognize the source of that awe beyond ourselves, the transcendent source that we participate in. Finding our own divinity requires deep looking. We may then reach an awareness of what the Buddhists call Buddha-nature or Christians call Christ-consciousness.

At the same time as we maintain a mind-set of giving glory, there needs to be recognition that God is extraordinarily ordinary, that is, embedded in the stuff of our daily lives. The sacred is not only in the overtly beautiful flowers and majestic mountains; it is present in the garbage that decomposes into rich soil, in the anger that can be transformed into constructive action, in the conflicts and tensions that can lead to creative outcomes. This is how the world becomes the way. I am reminded of the Buddhist instruction to spread your manure on the field of *bodhi* (the awakened place) so that seeds of enlightenment will sprout. We use the raw material of our lives to learn and to grow, and experience provides plenty of fertilizer.

I offer a small example from my own experience. Making my children's lunches was becoming a laborious and unwelcome task, especially at about one A.M., my usual time to approach it. For personal reasons, I wanted to do this for them (although they are both old enough to do it themselves), but I was simultaneously resenting it, wishing I could spend the time meditating instead. Finally, it occurred to me to turn the experience into a nightly lunch-making meditation. I give thanks for the slices of bread (noticing their texture and fragrance, thinking about where they come from, picturing the wheat field, the sun, rain, and soil necessary for their existence) and do the same for everything that goes between them. I notice the ingredients of the side dishes, even thanking the trees for the packaging, sometimes including the workers and machinery needed to provide it all. I touch the Source of these components and feel grateful. I think about the many mothers who don't have the opportunity to provide their children such nourishment and wish them the same good fortune I have. Some nights I muster more kavannah than others, but undoubtedly this infusion of mindfulness, gratitude, and sacredness into a seemingly mundane task has been beneficial. I recommend this kind of personal ritual, sacralizing the profane as a spiritual exercise.

It is my experience that a relationship with the Divine comes from doing, not intellectualizing. I'm reminded of the existentialist Søren Kierkegaard's pronouncement that the essence of religion is not to think a great thought but to risk a great love. Participating in the cosmic drama is necessary, with a sense of lifting up the heavens, alongside perfecting one's own soul. One climbs toward the Divine and, when the ladder is removed, God catches hold and pulls up those who somehow keep climbing. An attitude of receptivity is essential and requires practice. We have to work at opening this door to our consciousness; it is a discipline, a wrestling. But God dwells wherever we let Her in, so the sacred is potentially everywhere.

COVENANT–THE CONNECTING LINK

The first commandment of the Decalogue—"I am the Lord your God who brought you out of the land of Egypt, the house of bondage" (Exodus 20:2)—tells us that we were freed from slavery in order to enter into a covenantal life with God. We are given the freedom to be bound to God's law, which is an intriguing paradox that speaks to the marrow of real freedom. True liberation does not mean "anything goes." On the contrary, it is characterized by our willingness to lead a very regulated, morally ingrained life. In this willingness, we find the spaciousness of real freedom.

Inherent in the story is an interconnectedness between the redemptive act (that is, the role of the Deity) and our active participation in it. As the Book of Exodus unfolds, the midwives Shifrah and Puah refuse Pharaoh's order to slay the male Jewish children (Exodus 1:15–21). At great personal risk, they will not cooperate, and this act of disobedience is essential to the story's denouement. It illustrates the partnership we have with God (with the Source, the Way) in effecting our own salvation. The Jewish view of redemption is not one of passivity: In a sense, God saves those who save themselves, which is another paradox to be embraced, not understood. It involves free will and an openness to life's possibilities. This is part of liberation's spaciousness. When bound to moral law, we are given the freedom to resist immoral dictates. Such freedom results in courage and creativity. The midwives came up with an excuse that enabled them to continue their refusal: "These Hebrew women are so vigorous they give birth before we midwives even arrive." By "fearing God" (that is, trusting and respecting their own moral beliefs, which they experienced as sanctioned by God, taking refuge in them, revering them), they saved themselves and Moses.

Thus a covenantal relationship with the Deity is not a complacent position. It involves looking at the destructive elements in the socialized world around us and not being deceived by them. These elements are often much more subtle than Pharaoh's outrageous commands and require all our powers of discernment to recognize them. Such discernment means not being seduced by advertising that claims we have to look, smell, and act a certain way to be acceptable. It means not buying in to the worship of the dollar, of material goods as the vehicle to feeling valued. It means not succumbing to mindless entertainment that trivializes our existence, or addictions that consume us with toxins. These are all modern forms of slavery. Heschel makes a marvelous distinction between entertainment and celebration, noting that entertainment kills time, whereas celebration links us to eternity.

Embedded in the slave metaphor and the exodus, then, is the necessity of becoming aware of one's slave status. For the Hebrews, slavery in Egypt was the socialized world, and they resisted leaving it. Bondage itself can become addictive—one can cling to it (to use Buddhist terminology), wallow in it, revere it. It becomes familiar and comforting; we hesitate to let it go. Moses gave the Hebrews a vision of freedom and the words to move toward it, away from oppression's siren call. But first their consciousness had to be raised. In our society, we have to first become mindful that we are worshipping money, prestige, or fame, that we are shackled to the television set which preaches drinking the right beer to be lovable, that we are addicted to substances, work, or unhealthy relationships. This condition of alienation from an unfettered, authentic self, understood to have been created in God's image, is part and parcel of slavery. The result is adherence to a false self. James Finley, a student of Thomas Merton's, defines sin as "a tragic case of mistaken identity concerning our own selves." Sin, then, is a kind of oppression.

Liberation in Judaism is the metaphor for finding one's true self in the covenanted life with God. One learns to water the seeds of the yaetzer ha-tov—one's inherent inclination to goodness. Soul could be understood as the part of ourselves that is on its way to the true self. The world of blessed participation is part of this liberation, a world where we perceive the blessing in every aspect of life and say yes to it. Choosing freedom is indeed choosing life. It involves mindfulness and contemplation—a seeing that penetrates to a place of I-Thou relationship, a place of not perceiving people as objects and not perceiving ourselves as empty, worthless, and unlovable. We discover on the journey a need for centering to get in touch with this deeper self, to circumvent the socialization process that binds us. As Merton points out, this often involves embracing a certain amount of marginality, whether being a monk (or a rabbi), a social activist, or simply one unafraid to differ from the mainstream. I believe such liberation leads to faith. There is a midrash that the Red Sea did not separate until the first Jew threw himself into the water (or took that step beyond the nostril-level comfort zone). In my experience, we let go of servitude, take a leap, and the sea parts.

Three aspects of covenant suggest themselves for further examination. One is the personal relationship with God in Judaism. A second topic concerns the Jewish mystical side of this relationship in the form of *tikkun olam,* or "repair of the world." The third concerns Jewish ethics as a means of taking responsibility for our part in the covenant, by understanding and following the *mitzvot* (commandments) that lead to justice.

The Personal Experience of God in Judaism: Unraveling the G-Word

The theme of personal experience with God sings of Jewish

existentialism. By existentialism, I mean the celebration of the personal, the belief that our only way to know reality is to know it subjectively, that our individual experience in the here and now is, in fact, revelatory. Jews emphasize the capacity to connect directly with the Deity—to converse, complain, praise, argue, plead, give thanks, appreciate—all in the service of feeling connected.

I recently saw a play at the National Jewish Theatre called *Messiah*, whose central character (a seventeenth-century Polish woman with whom I felt an immediate identification) spends much of the drama in passionate conversations with God—questioning, consulting, confessing, raging. This, I feel, is the epitome of Buber's I-Thou relationship—a meeting of two subjects in a realm of deep recognition, openness, reciprocity. There was a distinct sense of dialogue rather than monologue in these communications. Rachel knew she was being heard and assumed a response would be forthcoming, even if it wasn't the one she was looking for. To feel unconditionally related to God is a way of coping with the fundamental angst of the human condition. Also to feel unconditionally loved and forgiven is an amazing concomitant of the relationship. The play touched on the unquenchable thirst for connection with transcendence in all our activities.

Of primary importance is that God should not be a stranger. Deuteronomy 6:5 states with stunning simplicity: "You shall love *Adonai* your God with all your heart and with all your soul and with all your might." It is impossible to love another without a deep knowing. So implicit in the exhortation to love is the injunction to know. It is through knowledge that deepens into love that the commandments become personal, when they come from a Being who is intimately known, in a context of love and mutuality.

Midrash maintains that it is our attention to the mitzvot that best expresses our love of the One in Whose name they are performed. I find Rosenzweig's distinction between law and commandment particularly compelling in relation to how love and mitzvot intermingle. He says that a law is impersonal, external, not directed to a "thou" or personalized other (anyone who exceeds the speed limit has broken the law); whereas a commandment is utterly personal, singular, and thou-directed: *Thou* shalt love, *thou* shalt not steal, etc. Thus the law is turned into a personally felt commandment. This happens only in the context of experience, however. Our consciousness shifts as we face situations that involve our own moral decisions or make us the recipient of the moral decisions of others. Rocky territories of cheating, stealing, adultery, lying, gossip, to name a few, become part of our own landscape. When we God-wrestle over issues of right and wrong, over correct conduct, we water seeds of divine involvement, and the resulting intimacy sends down deeper roots. Love blooms while the experience becomes internalized as caring command and the external law is no longer urgently needed.

Another aspect of Rosenzweig's approach to the mitzvot has felt particularly relevant to me. When asked whether he put on *tefillin* (the phylacteries mentioned earlier, which some observant Jews feel commanded to wear for prayer), he replied, "Not yet." He experienced himself as being in process as a Jew, and was aware of the necessity of being spiritually ready to incorporate a mitzvah. He neither berated himself for not adhering to the commandment nor closed off the possibility that one day he would observe it. This emphasis on finding authenticity in spiritual practice is the reverse of the rote ritual that can become so sterile. It gives one the space to discover meaning and to grow into one's practice.

Heschel uses the felicitous phrase "radical amazement" to describe the childlike sense of wonder one experiences when looking at the world as if for the first time. This sensibility is relevant to the personal encounter with God, an experience that strikes down deep at the root, that touches the mystery inherent in our contact with the transcendent realm. It is both exhilarating and frightening; it has an intensity that contains both joy and terror. Radical amazement is our response to the truly awesome nature of existence itself. When we perceive the God-saturated essence of all-that-is, we become filled with presence. In the language of some of our most astute philosophers and theologians of the past two centuries, we are participating in the mystery (Gabriel Marcel), intuiting the infinite (Friedrich Schleiermacher), encountering the Thou (Martin Buber), and finding our true selves (Thomas Merton). We are entering an open, spacious realm that contains both emptiness and fullness, where nothing is taken for granted. We are entering the present moment, where "getting a life" occurs *now*.

Such an orientation of presence makes it possible for us to understand something deeply by becoming one with it. This is an effective way of dealing with anger (or any strong emotion that threatens to become unmanageable or harmful); when we look deeply into it and know it, we develop the capacity to transform it. Thich Nhat Hanh uses the metaphor of "boiling the potatoes" of anger through meditation, to soften them and make them edible. The point is not to destroy the anger (or the *yaetzer*) but to alter its energy, transforming its destructive quality into something constructive. In the relationship with God, Who is beyond our rational understanding, our intimate connection also has the power of transformation, both for our own growth and, in some mysterious way, for God, Who benefits when we bring up the light, Whose power to give is perhaps enhanced by receiving our gifts. (See the next section on *tikkun*.)

My own experience of prayer accords very much with Thomas Moore (who writes so movingly about caring for our souls) in his response to a billboard that shouted: "Pray. It works." His billboard would announce: "Pray. It may not work." As Moore points out, very often what we think we want is the reverse of what we need. When we pray without expectations, with no strings attached except an authentic desire to connect to God, we open ourselves up to possibilities that transcend our limited understanding.

My suggestion to the spiritual seeker is simply to initiate the conversation. Chances are, God has been tapping you on the shoulder for some time, and you are now responding. Wherever you are comfortable, quiet, and alone, talk. Share whatever spontaneously arises, be it a worry, a question, an observation, a compliment, a song, even a joke. (Remember, God always gets the joke.) Keep the specific requests to a minimum, acknowledging that you don't know what is in your best interests. Instead, ask for guidance, clarity, support on the path, or ask for nothing but to feel God's presence. Learning to converse with God in your own language is immensely satisfying, but like anything worthwhile, it requires practice. Do it every day for a month. Don't be surprised if it is habit-forming. Some of my best conversations have been in the shower. (I find bathrooms to be much underrated, highly spiritual rooms.) Lately we connect in the car (but until you've become very familiar with it, don't pray and drive). Be receptive to the mutuality of this process, since God's replies are as varied as the universe. A response may come quickly, in the form of a thought, a physical sensation, an awareness, a dream. Or it may come later via another person, something you're drawn to read, or an occurrence in the natural environment. Discernment is helpful, but excessive cognition is an obstacle. Patience is required, and intuition is a necessity. Good luck (although luck has nothing to do with it)!

Tikkun and the Mystical Realm

Kabbalah is the word for the vast body of writings and discourse that constitute Jewish mysticism. Hundreds, perhaps thousands of volumes comprise Kabbalah, which means "that which has been received," a fitting commentary on our need to be receptive in order to witness the presence of Divine Reality. This aspect of covenant speaks to the human longing to be closer to God and the concomitant Divine longing to embrace humankind. The Kabbalistic view that creation and revelation occurred because God needs us, just as we need God, is startling. This suggestion of a mutuality in the human-Divine relationship despite the inequality enlarges the meaning of covenant and enriches our role as partners in it. These writings date back thousands of years, to Ezekiel's vision of the chariot in the Hebrew Scriptures, and extend up to the present time, as modern thinkers continue to probe the mysteries inherent in the experience of God. They contain myriad topics such as the intricacies of creation, what happened prior to creation, the existence of angels, the nature of man's soul, the hidden meaning of the 613 commandments in the Torah, as well as much emphasis on applying this theoretical knowledge in meditations designed to bring us closer to God, even to union with God.

Ordinary language fails when trying to explain mysticism. I prefer the words of the poet William Blake:

To see the world in a grain of sand
And heaven in a wild flower,
Hold infinity in the palm of your hand,
And eternity in an hour.

This is the realm of theosophy, which involves the direct experience of the Eternal, as opposed to theology, which uses stories, history, myth, and law to develop a system of beliefs about the relationship between God and man. Theosophy has the chutzpah (Yiddish for gall, guts, brazen nerve) to try to explore the mind of God.

I will share just a taste of what is so delicious to me in this realm. While the Kabbalists portray God as essentially unknowable and ineffable (as *Ein Sof*, meaning "without end" or "infinite"), they also describe Him/Her as having ten attributes or powers that emanated from the mysterious *Ein Sof* in creating the universe. The hidden God is paradoxically also the revealing God. These aspects of the personality of the Deity are called *Sefirot* (from the Hebrew word for "sapphire," referring to God's brightness) and are symbolized by the highest qualities in our human realm: wisdom, understanding, justice, and mercy, to name a few. Describing them in detail is beyond the scope of this essay. They relate to the concept of *tikkun*, or "repair of the universe," developed by a sixteenth-century Kabbalist named Isaac Luria. He wished to explain the nature of evil and to answer questions about why terrible traumas occur to undeserving people—a timeless dilemma, indeed. He came up with a theory of the creation of the world that involved God's exile (or *Tzimtzum*—the withdrawal of God to allow humankind to develop its own freedom and autonomy, to have free will) and the resulting "breaking of the vessels" that occurred after God's retreat. Here, the Sefirot are depicted as divine vessels of light that shattered when the world was being created. Some of the vessels were not strong enough to contain the light, thus the cosmic catastrophe that allowed broken fragments to enter our world. These bits of shattered light are encased in husks, called *kelipot*, which are the source of evil. It is our responsibility as human beings to rescue the scattered sparks and to return them to God. Thus, when we perform *tikkun olam*, we are reconstituting the universe; we are re-creating the species on a deeper level. We have a mandate to repair the broken fragments of the cosmos by doing *mitzvot*—commandments and good deeds. We also mend the world through prayer and meditation.

What I love about this explanation is that every word, deed, and thought is part of the process. By performing tikkun, by raising our consciousness to a higher level, we participate in making God whole again; we are partners in the redemption of the world. In this frame of thought, everything has cosmic significance, like the "butterfly effect" in physics (which maintains that when even so small a creature as a butterfly on earth flaps its wing, the effect is felt throughout the universe), or karma in Eastern religion (where every action has a corresponding reaction—cause and effect). Tikkun thus contains an ethical imperative: How we live matters. For a Jew, part of the goal is to be a lover of life. There is a responsibility to be joyful and to appreciate life's pleasures, which, like God's holy sparks, permeate all of creation. This need for joy and appreciation feels resoundingly true to me.

The *Sheckinah* (that divine feminine Presence in my poem, Who is also one of the Sefirot) is said to rest on the ark where the Torah is kept and is especially present on Shabbat, the Jewish Sabbath. (She is also known as the Sabbath Queen.) She is the aspect of God Who is in exile with us. Jewish mysticism calls for a necessary reunion of the masculine and feminine aspects of God into One, symbolized by sexual union, which (as mentioned before) is considered a mitzvah for a man and his wife on Shabbat. Since every action on earth has its celestial counterpart, such physical lovemaking helps to unite the *sefirah* (singular of *sefirot*) *Tiferet* (beauty, seen as a masculine dimension) with the feminine *Sheckinah*. Far from being sinful, sex (under the right circumstances) is a moral imperative.

So what should be our response to suffering in the world? The mystical tradition says it is tikkun—mending the broken world through the sacredness of all we do. It is not only an activist position; it calls for a transformation of consciousness. And it is felt in the universe. This is similar to the Buddhist notion that you can go into a closet and change your mind on an issue, and that shift alone makes a difference, even before you've left the closet. Here the essence of spirituality is the quality of one's response, one's kavannah, or sacred intent, that should accompany a religious act, which can be any act.

My first experience of kavannah in a Jewish context was an encounter with a rabbi who was officiating at a bat mitzvah I attended, an ordinary event for him but a truly extraordinary one in my eyes. This man, Rabbi Douglas Goldhamer, exuded a kind of spiritual charisma that pervaded the room and touched me at my core. He conveyed a deep inwardness, concentration, devotion in his relationship to the service, the Torah, the young woman. I came away feeling astonished to have had a religious experience in a synagogue. The impact ultimately changed my life. I began studying Jewish mysticism with him (an area in which he has great interest and expertise) and three years later became a rabbinical student in his newly formed Hebrew Seminary of the Deaf. To have found a rabbi who practices *Jewish* meditation, who is a healer, and who regards my spiritual experiences as gifts rather than abnormalities has been an enormous blessing.

A profound opposition exists between the rational and mystical traditions in Judaism, but the possibility of synthesis is also profound because the two strands need each other. I live this opposition in my own household. I am very drawn to mystical thinking, to involvement with the transrational realm, the experience of the Divine, of angels, miracles, synchronicities; I maintain a devoted receptivity to the extraordinary quality of ordinary life. My husband is the embodiment of Rational Man; he is a scientist, a radiologist for whom seeing is believing and who exemplifies intense skepticism toward this mysterious realm. He is a devout atheist who finds my spiritual endeavors both puzzling and sometimes painful. He is also one of the most decent, ethical human beings I have ever known. If we can learn to dialogue (as we have been struggling to do), to live peacefully and lovingly together with our differences, and to respect one another despite them, we will have learned a lot about conflict resolution. I believe the effort is truly an act of *tikkun*. Perhaps one day we can be advisors to the Mideast peace talks.

The concept of tikkun relates to the optimistic strain of postmodernism, which deconstructs reality but finds meaning in the fragments rather than despair. The meaningful fragments are like the broken tablets that, according to Midrash, stayed in the ark after Moses smashed them (thus the title of Gilman's book *Sacred Fragments*). The commandments were broken, but not meaningless. They connect to the symbol of the shattered vessels; they too link us to the Divine. Existentialists like Rosenzweig, Buber, and Heschel exemplify this optimistic strain of thought; they see the fragments as revelatory. This is not a world of neat, rational consistency, but it is a world where a relationship to a Presence that is both transcendent and immanent is an absorbing and meaningful possibility.

It is empowering to feel that we have responsibility for what happens in the world, that we are in a profound partnership with God. It is also awesome. Neither are we passive recipients of God's goodness nor need we be passive victims of the world's cruelty. We must learn to embrace the mystery of this partnership by participating as fully as possible in it, by accepting the "secure insecurity" (Buber's term) of it.

To consciously practice tikkun (which you probably have been doing in other ways without knowing it), take an area of conflict in your life and sit with it in contemplation. Let the agitation around it settle down, like dirt in a glass of water. It could take several "sittings" to achieve this more relaxed state. Ask God to give you greater clarity in how to approach the conflict with integrity and compassion. Empty yourself of preconceived notions of how to proceed; open yourself to Her guidance in the matter. Focus on your breath to quiet the agitation; rather than clamping down on thoughts or feelings, let them float through like clouds in the sky of your mind. In this emptied, receptive state you are most capable of hearing the soundless voice of God, subtly directing you as to how to retrieve the holy sparks. When you bring harmony into your personal life, you are helping to repair the universe.

Waging Justice Through Ethics—The Role of Mishpat

Social justice, which involves both lawmaking and compassion, has such a strong emphasis in Jewish teachings that some designate it the genius of the Hebrew Scriptures. A central tenet is the importance of a just society and the formation of rules to live by, known as a *mishpat*, so as to create a just society. Judaism thus contains a strong commitment to aiding the downtrodden, the oppressed, the vulnerable person; to giving clothing, food, shelter, and respect to those in need. This adherence to ethical living becomes a cornerstone of the covenant with God. In order to remain in right relationship to the Divine, we are obligated to study, internalize, and implement His commandments. All religious activity is judged by the extent to which it establishes mishpat in the community. There is a focus on the treatment of the other, especially the marginalized other—the stranger, the widow, the orphan, the imprisoned.

Again and again we're advised to remember that we were once

strangers in Egypt and to act on that collective memory so as not to do to others the wrong that was done to us. This is more difficult than it sounds, for without awareness, the natural inclination often is to do precisely what was done to us (which is why child abuse is so cyclical). Always, mindfulness is essential in the process.

The *Sh'ma* is the inspirational Jewish monotheistic credo recited morning and night and at times of crisis. It is usually translated, "Hear, O Israel! The Lord our God, the Lord is One!" I prefer the translation at Congregation Bene Shalom, the temple of the Jewish deaf: "Pay attention people of Israel: The Lord our God, the Lord is One!" This call to mindfulness is punctuated by two claps of the hands while saying "Pay attention," which really does capture one's attention. We're reminded to wake up to the awareness that God is One, just as remembering Egypt encourages us not to repeat the experience of oppression but to have empathy for those who suffer from it. Both reminders refer to the basic oneness of all-that-is, a perception that deepens compassion for one's companions.

Mishpat is a tough-minded teaching, stressing fairness and the importance of correct judgments. It relates to the sefirah or aspect of the deity called *gevurah*, which roughly translated is "tough love," as opposed to *chesed*, the sefirah or aspect that could be regarded as unconditional love. Or one could translate them respectively as "judgment" and "mercy." Yet I see fair judgments as necessarily containing a great deal of compassion. As the biblical injunction "to do justly, love mercy, and walk humbly with your God" (Micah 6:8) suggests, how can one do justly without loving mercy?

Waging justice is a Jewish way of expressing interconnected-ness. Unique as we each are, we are also interrelated in a matrix of being. No matter how well off we are materially, we are com-manded to remain experientially connected to the poor, the oppressed, and the outcast, and this enables us to promote justice and righteousness. While Jews have been branded pejoratively by some as "liberal do-gooders," opposing exploitation, societal evil, and corruption is a spiritual mission in Judaism. Such social action comes from a very deep place in the tradition. Injustice is actually viewed as an affront to God.

The question could be raised, "Why does God allow injustice?" One answer is that righteous individuals (the *tzadikim*) live by their faith, understanding that free will is intrinsic to God's plan. Alongside performing good deeds, then, the righteous person must have faith that injustice is temporal and eventually will be redressed ("eventually" stretching into a more atemporal realm of many lifetimes). The commandment of *tzedakah* is connected to the notion of justice. Much more than charity, tzedakah encompasses this deep sense of righteousness that embodies faith and action. It suggests living in a God-centered way. Thus another person's material welfare is our spiritual concern. There is an emphasis on community here, on caring for one another. The life of the community may depend on this, as the story of Sodom and Gomorrah in the Book of Genesis so graphically demonstrates. Ten tzadikim could have saved their communities. One wonders whether ten tzadikim could have had any impact on Nazi Germany, or whether, in fact, ultimately they did. The message is resounding: Even when surrounded by corruption of the worst kind (especially then, perhaps), we have an obligation to lead God-centered lives.

What does it mean to lead a God-centered life? Perhaps the answer to this question is the core of covenant. In chapter 19 of the Book of Leviticus we are urged to imitate God and become holy ourselves: "You shall be holy, for I, the Lord your God, am holy" (*K'doshim tih'yu ki kadosh ani Adonai Eloheikhem*) (19:2). The Hebrew word *kadosh* is only roughly equivalent to the English word *holy*. It is a word that implies separation, a division between the sacred and the profane, paradoxical in a tradition that also strives to sacralize the profane. While *kadosh* often is used to characterize God, it also applies to places, times, objects, and procedures connected with sacredness. Gradually, *kadosh* came to mean the spiritual gap between human fallibility and divine perfection. Thus the feeling of inadequacy that can come over us at times within the awesomeness of God's Presence. Yet our tradition makes it clear that despite the gap, God is approachable and available—another paradox to be embraced holistically. In this magnificent chapter of the Torah, right conduct reaches its pinnacle, both in the verse just quoted and in verse 18, which is probably the most widely quoted commandment in the Hebrew Scriptures: "Love your neighbor as yourself."

This commandment may be as close as one can come to an answer to what constitutes God-centeredness in Judaism. It is aptly named "the golden rule." The Talmudic sage Hillel expressed it in the negative to a man who asked to be taught Torah while standing on one foot: "What is hateful to you, you do not do to your neighbor. That is the whole Torah; the rest is commentary. Go and learn." The thousands of volumes comprising the commentary speak to the complexity of the issue. The precept has been a source of wisdom for teachers and philosophers from Confucius to Kant. Jesus of Nazareth felt that it was second in importance only to the command to love God. Rabbi Akiba (another Talmudic sage) called it "the great principle of the Torah." It relates to that "higher portion" of God that reaches beyond *halacha* (or law) because it cannot be legislated. In its practice, we are probably being as holy and Godlike as our human capacity permits.

To the many distinguished commentaries that have addressed this golden commandment, I add my own thoughts on the subject. I raise the question why the commandment is not first to love ourselves; that is, to be mindful of the spark of divinity that is our essence, having been created in God's image. The premise that man is partial to himself contains a significant shadow element, whereby that partiality can be transformed into its opposite. Thus in my experience (both as a psychotherapist and as an observer), self-loathing alongside self-doubt, distrust, and shame is of such epidemic proportions that it seems of little value to instruct someone to love others as oneself until one's self has been adequately loved. A fundamental sense of unworthiness has pervaded large segments of humankind. Depression, anxiety states, and many forms of addiction currently plague our society. Truly, we are in a crisis of unloved selves.

Surely it behooves us to nurture and tend our inner gardens, to take pleasure in our accomplishments, to be the artists and poets of our own lives. As we learn to appreciate our own Divine image, I believe we will be more available to help our neighbor in times of need. Loving kindness, that most sought-after and elusive of attributes, flows naturally and abundantly from those who have discovered themselves to be beloved souls.

CONCLUSION

As the previous pages have suggested, the spiritual path is a wilderness journey that develops and deepens over time. The Jewish oases of Torah, ritual, and covenant, with their many interwoven themes, provide sustenance that enables the traveler to establish that "secure insecurity" Buber refers to as probably the steadiest balance available. The path is one of accepting uncertainty, appreciating ambiguity, and acknowledging impermanence in our human realm. Torah shines as our central symbol, ritual is the enactment of the symbol, and covenant is the glue that holds us together. Other traditions have their own necessary way stations in the desert, equally worthy in their followers' quest for Eternal Truth.

Following Ron Miller's outline of an unfolding spirituality has been particularly helpful to me. The process begins with seeking answers and finding them. Then comes questioning and wrestling with those answers that may have given comfort at an earlier phase. Next (or perhaps simultaneously) comes a sense of marveling over the whole landscape. The final stage allows for resting in the very ambiguities that once led to such doubts and fears.

Clearly, as one's understanding matures, there is less satisfaction with previously acceptable answers to questions such as what is eternal, where is God, how do we lead meaningful lives. One can look to the biblical wrestlers for inspiration: Abraham, Jacob, Moses, Job. I assume there were lady wrestlers too, but we have less information about them. Sarah must have wrestled with Hagar (her handmaid and husband's mistress). Rebecca struggled with her predilection for Jacob over Esau. And Rachel contended with con- flicting views about God, surreptitiously carrying her father's household idols when she left home with Jacob, just in case. But mostly we learn about wrestling from the sweat of our own experi- ence. Our lives provide so many opportunities for challenging and confronting God alongside the big questions.

Out of the struggle comes excitement that leads to a sense of wonder. Again, Heschel's "radical amazement" comes to mind. It describes exactly my response to being in a rabbinical seminary at this point in my life after so much searching—the gratitude and astonishment. I want to laugh out of sheer delight and perplexity at the twists and turns my life has taken. That awe is a fundamental ingredient of our participation in the mystery of existence feels pro- foundly true to me.

Finally comes some sense of control in the process, which para- doxically must come from an attitude of passionate surrender. I say this having only glimpsed this place on the path in an occasional flash of clarity, therefore having much less familiarity with it than the other stages. It is a resting place, but not one of complacency. I imagine it must be born of wisdom and compassion. I assume we become more mindful but less self-conscious, more rooted in God. We somehow put our egos to death and let our selves be born. Such resting or reigning involves an integration of all our parts into a meaningful whole—this is shalom, which means not only hello, good-bye, and peace, but also wholeness, completeness. We have control of our lives only to the extent that we acknowledge our inevitable deaths as necessary, as vital to wholeness.

Spirituality, then, could be viewed as the road to shalom. We wonder if we'll ever arrive there. Our primary focus, however, must be on the practice of spirituality, not the outcome. Our day-to-day activity is the link to Ultimate Reality, which is so much broader than organized religion. I ask myself: What do I *do* as a Jew? I answer, I study Torah, Hebrew, Kabbalah. Study is a form of prayer. I talk to God—directly, intimately, regularly. I meditate to know myself better, to be more receptive to God's replies. I write poetry to express my gratitude and wonder or my outrage and confusion depending on the moment. I use what I learn to relate as compassionately and lovingly as possible to my neighbor, whom I recognize as a beloved soul, like myself. With regard to the many mitzvot I do not observe, I say, "Not yet. Maybe someday." Meanwhile, I live life with as much blessed participation as I can muster.

The spiritual path is an individual path walked one step at a time in solitary fashion. While good guidance and companionship are critical along the way, ultimately we make our own footprints. Authenticity in the choices we make is an essential ingredient that involves knowing ourselves well, developing discernment in relation to others, and trusting our intuition to help connect us to the Source beyond ourselves. To all the readers of these pages who are seeking answers, finding them, wrestling with them, and marveling over the mystery, I wish you shalom.

DEFINING ENLIGHTENMENT

Judith Blackstone

A SPECIFIC PHASE OF MATURITY

Life has meaning because it has direction. It has a goal. Most of us create meaning in our lives by creating goals for ourselves such as family, wealth, artistic achievement. But life has a goal that we don't have to create, that is inherent in its nature, in our nature. Our own personal life evolves towards a specific destination that is sometimes called self-realization, or enlightenment. Just as our created goals are based on our desire for something, we also have a fundamental desire for life's inherent goal. It is this underlying desire for enlightenment that often causes us to feel unfulfilled, even after we have achieved our created goals.

The word *enlightenment* often is used in a general way to describe a variety of experiences. In my definition, which is similar to that of most Eastern religious teachings, enlightenment refers to a specific phase of human maturity, a specific and unmistakable shift in the way one experiences life.

Although enlightenment is the most concrete, actual experience of being alive, describing it always sounds abstract, until you have experienced it yourself.

To understand the relationship of enlightenment and self, and how they both mature at the same time, we need to clearly understand the specific experiences that are meant by the words *enlightenment* and *self*. The following definitions are based on my own experience, on the experience of friends and students, and on the definitions found in the spiritual texts of Buddhism and Hinduism. The point I wish to emphasize is that the definitions offered here are not solely from my subjective experience (for then they could certainly be fantasy) and are also not solely the paraphrasing of long-dead sages from old books (for they might be naive or metaphorical). Rather, they are descriptions that many people agree on, based on their own experience, that support the validity of the ancient texts.

REALIZATION OF FUNDAMENTAL CONSCIOUSNESS

Enlightenment is the realization, the lived experience, that we are made of pure consciousness; that pure consciousness is our fundamental nature and our ultimate reality; and that everything else in the universe is also made of pure consciousness, so that our own being is fundamentally unified with all of nature. As one fourth-century Chinese sage put it, "Everything in the universe is one and the same root as my own self." In enlightenment, we experience life from the vantage point of that root.

We experience our own self as unbroken consciousness, pervading our body and our environment. This means that there is a continuity between our inner and outer perception. We have a sense of vast space, as if all our perceptions were one single tapestry of reflections in a single mirror. We feel that we are made of clear, empty space, finer than air, unbounded and motionless. Within this vast space moves the changing progression of our thoughts, feelings, sensations, and perceptions.

I call this unbroken, pervasive dimension "fundamental consciousness." Before we realize fundamental consciousness, we identify ourselves as our sensations, feelings, perceptions, ideas, memories. But when we realize fundamental consciousness, we recognize that these discrete, transitory experiences come and go within the fundamental ground that is our true identity.

When people begin to realize fundamental consciousness, they report that they feel translucent, or permeable. One man told me excitedly that he had discovered that the world was round, because he could now experience the space behind him and to the sides of him, rather than just in front of him. The shift from our frontal self-object relationship with the world to an experience of continuity with the world affects every aspect of our lives, including our ability to understand and to love; even our physical health. One woman told me that before her realization, she felt that she was watching life; now she felt she was participating. Experiencing a continuity with the world, she felt a basic kinship with everything she encountered. And because she experienced her inner responses at the same time as she experienced the outer world, she felt engaged in the encounters.

BECOMING REAL

Consciousness is our ultimate reality. In Hindu metaphysics, ultimate reality is called by the Sanskrit word *Brahman* and described like this: "I am the supreme Brahman which is pure consciousness, always clearly manifest, unborn, one only, imperishable, unattached and all-pervading and nondual." Although this description, from the ninth-century Indian philosopher Shankara, may sound exotic or abstract, every word is soberly meant as a description of the fundamental reality of every human being. Reality is the opposite of abstract. It is real.

In enlightenment, we experience that we are becoming real; not something new, but something we have always been yet only barely known. This is what Shankara means by unborn: the unified, pervasive, pure consciousness has always been there, pervading our every cell. It is the true, whole "I" that is our inherent, fundamental nature, hidden behind the partial, fragmented, abstract "I's" that we tolerate before we know of our wholeness. We do not have to create reality; it has always been there. But the ability to recognize reality is also inherent in us. All our lives we have been guided by our ability to tell truth from deception, balance from disharmony. As we realize fundamental consciousness, we recognize that our underlying reality has been the goal of our lifelong navigation and desire.

Enlightenment is an experience unlike any other we have had because there is no duality in it. We do not have an experience *of* fundamental consciousness. Although the limits of language make it necessary for us to use the preposition *of*, fundamental consciousness is actually realizing itself. It is self-reflecting. The knower and the known are the same. Fundamental consciousness is our own ordinary consciousness, but directly, purely experienced, without the usual veils of habit, confusions, and defense. Enlightenment is the phase of human maturity in which the mind comes to know itself.

The state of continuity within ourselves, and between ourselves and our environment, is our inherent, and actually most normal, state. Several people have expressed fear to me about who they will become if they allow themselves to become enlightened. But once they have realized fundamental consciousness, they see that they have only become themselves, a deeply familiar and instantly recognizable being.

MISCONCEPTIONS

Enlightenment is much easier to experience than most people think. I've watched people stomp angrily out of workshops because I was asking them to experience what revered masters have experienced, as if the attempt were futile and even sacrilegious. I want to emphasize that *enlightenment* is a relative term. A

Zen master once told me, "Enlightenment is easy to achieve. But to realize it completely can take many lifetimes." In this way, it is something like being pregnant. You can be a little bit pregnant and no one would say that you are not "really" pregnant, but you have not yet come to full term. There is a tremendous range between the advanced enlightenment of the masters and the bit of enlightenment of which we are all capable. When we first become enlightened, we have begun a phase of maturity that potentially stretches far ahead of us. But the beginning of enlightenment is accessible to anyone who is interested in it.

There is also a tendency for us to impose the sense of sanctity that some of us were taught in Judeo-Christian tradition onto these principles of enlightenment. Much of Western religion teaches an attitude of reverence and humility towards a distant god, an image of patriarchal authority that we can petition but never truly know. Religious students are treated as children who can sit in the protective, vigilant presence of God, but who have only the responsibility of obedience. In the more ritualistic forms of Eastern religion as well, there is a hushed, hallowed quality when discussing the ultimate, and certainly there is great respect shown for the spiritual masters.

But the more advanced the teaching, and the students, become, the more the ultimate is presented as something belonging to us, as a wonderful but entirely usual part of our own nature, that can neither be taken away nor given to us by any external presence. I have found that many people who are ready for enlightenment are not achieving it because they assume it is some far-distant, exalted state. The work that so many of us have been doing to become more real, more open to life, has been leading towards the realization of our fundamental dimension of consciousness. It is crucial to our personal growth that we recognize our essential reality and demystify our understanding of enlightenment.

Another related misconception about enlightenment is that it is an "altered" state of consciousness. Enlightenment often is confused with the peak experiences that many people have, for example, while looking up at the stars or witnessing the birth of a baby. But a peak experience is by definition a momentary event, often accompanied by intense emotions such as awe or ecstasy. Enlightenment is not a momentary alteration of consciousness that one goes to and returns from. For this same reason, it also differs from the state of being hypnotized and the trance state. Enlightenment is a clear, alert perception of the present moment that represents a lasting refinement of consciousness.

Some people do have their first entry into enlightenment as a peak experience, a satori, during which they are dazzled by the sudden shift into the unity of fundamental consciousness. And some have had sudden deepenings of enlightenment as well, in which they abruptly experience much more of the space of fundamental consciousness than before. But enlightenment itself is not a temporary nor a particularly charged emotional state. It is a lasting transformation of our being, involving our ongoing relation to ourselves and our environment.

Sometimes enlightenment is said to be instantaneous because there is a definitive difference between being in the dimension of fundamental consciousness and not being in it. Some people notice this difference suddenly, while others, once they do notice it, feel that they have been there for a while without registering or naming it. One may lose the realization of fundamental consciousness and get it back several times before it becomes stable. But once we do become stable in our realization, we continue to live there, while our realization very gradually deepens and expands.

This means that our experience of fundamental consciousness gradually pervades more of our body, increasing our sense of inner depth and wholeness and opening new realms of sensitivity and insight. And it gradually increases our sense of oneness with other people, with nature, and with the cosmos. The most advanced spiritual masters, those rare few who are completely, or almost completely, enlightened, are said to be omniscient and omnipresent. They have realized the entire ground of fundamental consciousness, pervading the whole universe.

One point that sometimes causes confusion about the gradual, relative nature of enlightenment is that Buddhist teachers make a distinction between what they call gradual or progressive enlightenment and direct or sudden enlightenment. But these terms refer to two methods used to evoke the initial realization itself. They do not refer to the subsequent *process* of deepening and broadening one's realization. The Buddhist term "sudden enlightenment" does not mean that we realize the entire ground of fundamental consciousness all at once.

Sometimes the question is asked: Why do we have to work to achieve the realization of a dimension that is naturally part of ourselves? The Buddha taught that we are already enlightened; we are just not aware of it. But why not? Zen Buddhism speaks of our "beginningless greed, anger, and ignorance" that separate us from the recognition of our true nature. Hinduism points to an accumulation over many lifetimes of confusion and attachments that pull us outward from our true self and obscure the basic purity of our consciousness. This explanation also puts the beginning of our trouble in the unfathomable past. And the Bible offers its own Rorschach-like allegory of our fall from grace in the Garden.

One thing is clear. We are not born enlightened. Children, although undefended, are not experiencing the whole of the dimension of fundamental consciousness. There is a vast difference between the openness and unguarded love of an infant and the far-reaching clarity and intense but detached love of a spiritual master. As adults, we must grow towards enlightenment as well as release the psychological defenses that impede this growth. Although there is much literature on what separates us from fundamental consciousness, the question of why we must work to realize what has been there all along remains unanswered.

ENLIGHTENMENT IS UNITY

To become enlightened is to move from a fragmented experience of life to a unified experience. Before we become enlightened, our focus shifts from self to object, or from one modality of experience to another. We may experience another person quite fully but be only barely aware of ourselves. In another moment, we know our own feelings but our perception of the outside world is diminished. Or we may know our thoughts but not be conscious of our feelings or sensations.

When we become enlightened, we have realized the continuity, the unity, of inner and outer consciousness without any shifting of focus. This means that there is no longer any divisive schism between subject and object or between thought, feeling, and sensation. For example, at this moment, sitting at my typewriter, I am aware of the objects around me (their form and texture), including the window in front of my desk and the bit of earth and tree trunk I can see while looking down at my work. I am aware of the sensation of being in my body, of the emotional content of the moment (even though there is no particular emotional charge at the moment, there is still an emotional tone that is always present), and of the intensity of my mental activity. All these perceptions are unmistakably a whole; they exist in a single unbounded space, and the space itself has a luminous, vibrant quality. This is nonduality. I and other become one whole in the one pervasive field of fundamental consciousness.

This wholeness of I and other does not negate the integrity of the individual wholeness of each person or object. In fact, our individual boundaries are more defined in the dimension of fundamental consciousness. Once we can experience our own inner life at the same time as we experience the outer world, it becomes very clear where we leave off and the world begins.

DIRECT EXPERIENCE

To become enlightened is to experience life directly, without the interference of psychological defenses, projections, and preconceptions, and without the distraction of our habitual mental chatter. As fundamental consciousness, we pervade both the subject and the object of experience, the perceiver and the perceived. We thus experience no barrier, no gap, between ourselves and our experience.

For example, a woman had worked with me for two years and thoroughly explored her childhood history, releasing much of the pain of growing up in a chaotic, alcoholic family. One day, she came to the session in tears, saying that she had just realized that she had been seeing her life "through a filter." She said that she had suddenly caught a glimpse of herself in the mirror and realized that she had not been seeing herself as she really is. She had either superimposed an image of herself on the reflection in the mirror, based on a fashion-magazine ideal, or she had seen herself as her feared, negative image of herself, misshapen and homely. She had been afraid to see herself directly, without the filter. She also realized that she was not seeing her husband clearly, or the other important people in her life. She was afraid that if she saw them directly, either she would see that they did not really love her, or she would see something that she did not like and she would reject them. Yet she felt that much of her social awkwardness arose from the fact that she was not seeing people as they truly are, but rather idealizing or diminishing them.

This filter is actually typical of the human condition, but not many people ever notice it. As we realize fundamental consciousness, we see through the veils of our projections and defenses to experience life as it really is.

There is a Zen story, one version of which goes as follows: A monk and his teacher are walking in the teacher's garden. The monk asks his teacher to explain the phrase "The whole universe is of one and the same root as my own self." The teacher points to a rose and says, "Most people see this flower as if they were in a dream." I believe that the dream the teacher refers to is the cloudiness of our consciousness that separates us from our direct experience of life.

When we are not enlightened, we live abstractly, in our idea of life. Instead of seeing this particular flower, we see a general flower, like an image from a file in our minds marked "flower." And our flower file may be full of memories and associations that cause us to respond to the flower with feelings that are not directly related to this particular flower. In other words, we respond in a distorted or diminished way to our distorted or diminished perception of the world.

Our abstract perception of the world is to some degree a fantasy, and whether it is a romance or a horror story, it is not as satisfying as the direct experience of life. When we realize fundamental consciousness, we begin to truly see, truly touch, truly hear. We move from abstraction to substance, from imagination to actuality.

Many people fear that the actual world will be dull and ugly compared to their abstract dream-life. But our senses, when (relatively) unfettered by psychological defense and fantasy, reveal a more vivid, more balanced world than we ever imagined. If we are seeing a preconceived flower, a composite of many past flowers, we will not notice the richness of color, softness of texture, exact form of the present flower, and we certainly will not see the subtle radiance that surrounds the flower, that matches the light of our own aliveness. We will not notice that the flower is pervaded by the same radiant emptiness that pervades our own body; we will not notice that we are inseparably unified with the flower in the emptiness of pure consciousness that is the root of all things in the universe.

In enlightenment, our senses become unified. We experience life as a unified field of energy, vibrating in a unified field of pure, empty consciousness. This vibration is registered by all of our senses at once. We have a single, unified impression of life that is seen, heard, touched (felt), smelled, tasted, all at the same time. This adds fullness and resonance to all our experience. For example, when we perceive the aliveness inside a branch of a tree, in the dimension of fundamental consciousness, we experience that we are seeing-feeling-hearing it. The poet Rainer Maria Rilke describes this unified perception when he thanks the mythic musician Orpheus for "creating a tree in the ear." Rilke's Orpheus is attuned to the subtle foundation of life in which the visible world is audible and the audible world is visible.

The eyes are one of the most defended parts of the body. If we do not relax our seeing, then our way of looking at the world will keep us in the fragmented condition of I and other, rather than the unity, or continuity, of I and other that is experienced in fundamental consciousness. In order to live in this unified dimension, we need to allow the visual images around us to exist as they really are, without defending against them. To experience life directly, we need to receive the world in the empty, unobstructed field of fundamental consciousness, just as it is.

REALIZATION OF THE ETERNAL

The dimension of fundamental consciousness never changes. When we realize this most subtle dimension of ourselves, we experience a vast, unchanging stillness pervading our body and our environment. We feel that we ourselves are fundamentally timeless and changeless. Zen Buddhism expresses this with the phrase, "I have never moved from the beginning."

Yet the life that occurs within our fundamental consciousness is all movement and change. All the systems that make up our being, such as our blood, our nerve impulses, our stream of mental associations, our meridians of subtle energy, as well as the flow of circumstances in our lives, are in constant motion. The more we experience the absolute stillness of fundamental consciousness, the more freely and efficiently the movement of life takes place. We become healthier physically; we respond more deeply emotionally; and our thinking becomes clearer and more creative.

If you were attuned to fundamental consciousness, you would feel streamings of energy inside your body. Like fundamental consciousness, energy is an essential aspect of ourselves and the cosmos. The more open we are to life (the less defended we are psychologically), the more energy we feel in our bodies.

Although energy is an essential aspect of our nature for the duration of our growth towards wholeness, it is not our ultimate reality. Hindu metaphysics says that energy is a condensation or contraction of pure consciousness, and physical matter is a condensation of energy. It is the imbalance created by this mysterious contraction of pure consciousness that produces the dynamic flux, the myriad cycles, the creative chaos and sexy friction, the war and illness or vague discomfort that is our life on this planet. Hindu metaphysics also teaches that in complete enlightenment we accomplish a balance that is again pure consciousness, and we are no longer reborn in the world of energy and matter.

In our phenomenal world, pure consciousness pervades energy and physical matter, and energy pervades physical matter. Many people practicing spiritual and therapeutic disciplines reach the dimension of energy before they realize fundamental consciousness. The shift into the experience of oneself as energy from the experience of oneself as only physical matter, or only mental concepts, is so radical and liberating that many people assume they have reached the ultimate dimension of existence. It is important for our continuing maturity that we understand that fundamental consciousness is primary and pervades the energy in our body and in the cosmos. The cultivation of energy without the realization of fundamental consciousness can exacerbate our imbalance and discomfort.

When we have a lot of energy in our bodies but have not yet realized fundamental consciousness, we often feel overwhelmed by our own energy and the energy in the environment. The realization of fundamental consciousness grounds us in our true sense of self and centers us in the vertical core of our bodies. If we experience our own nature as the clear, unchanging stillness of fundamental consciousness, our energy can move freely through our stillness without overwhelming us. One student told me she no longer felt like a "walking whirlwind," manipulated and disoriented by powerful inner and outer currents.

There are techniques for protecting ourselves from unwanted influences in the energy dimension, but these involve holding an image of a surrounding light or other protective boundary. These techniques diminish our direct experience of life because they involve a constant use of the imagination, and they also promote an attitude of fearfulness. They are not necessary when we live in the dimension of fundamental consciousness. For example, a woman came to see me who had lived in a spiritual community for many years. She had recently stopped her meditation practice because she had had an experience that badly frightened her. She had felt such overpowering waves of love during her meditation that she was afraid she would go crazy if she allowed them to continue. When she learned how to attune to fundamental consciousness, she was able to let the waves of love pass through the unmoving space of her consciousness without disturbing it. She experienced herself as steady and stable, and at the same time, she experienced the streaming energy of her open heart.

Once we are secure in our realization of fundamental consciousness, we can open without fear to our own energy and the energy around us. We are like an empty vessel. Whatever is in the vessel is temporary and does not alter our fundamental nature. No matter how powerful the movement of life becomes, it does not change the absolute stillness of fundamental consciousness.

This is the paradox of enlightenment. We receive the stimulation of our environment even more fully than before we were enlightened. Because we have more access to the depths of ourselves, we feel everything, joy and pain, more deeply than before. But at the same time, we experience ourselves as whole and steady, as the unchanging ground of fundamental consciousness. One of my teachers once likened this state to the biblical burning bush. "We burn," he said, "but we are not consumed."

Our emotional pain is secondary to our fundamental nature. No matter what we lose or suffer in our life, this core of our being, our true reality, cannot be damaged. It has not moved from the beginning, and it will never move. Thus, as we become enlightened, it is easier to be at peace with even the worst of our circumstances. We can allow ourselves to mourn or rage, to risk new relationships and situations, because we know that our fundamental nature will always survive.

SUMMARY

In summary, enlightenment is the realization of one's own nature as ultimate reality. It is a radical shift from the fragmentation of subject-object duality to the unity of our fundamental dimension of pure consciousness. This fundamental dimension is experienced as vast, clear, unbreakable, unbounded space, pervading both our body and our environment. Once we realize fundamental consciousness, our realization continues to deepen and expand throughout our lifetime. When we become enlightened, our own mind is continuous with the consciousness that is the basis of all existence, which has been its true nature all along. Our dimension of fundamental consciousness is always with us, at the root of our self and the universe, and we are all capable of realizing it.

THE FAITH BEYOND THE FAITHS

Robert Granat

"REALISM"

The momentous moment has arrived at last—just when we, of all people, are here to greet it! History has been building up to this since prehistory, and evolution has been working toward it for eons. In our time, for the first time, that vast and forbidding world of theirs has suddenly shrunk, leaving us with this small and vulnerable planet of ours. All those long-separate spheres of cultural, racial, and geographical solidarity are crowded together and rubbing against each other; their surface tensions have ruptured and they are deliquescing, coalescing, into one, with startling swiftness like globules of mercury. Almost everybody senses something special is happening now, though hardly anybody knows exactly what—or what to make of it. Most people don't talk about it—or won't. Understandably too, because this great birthing is too agonizing, is bringing along so much dying. Look around—not just at the soft and rotting places; anywhere. You no longer need a poet's prescience to see that the centers aren't holding and things are falling apart. Every evening we can watch the ceremonies of innocence being drowned and mere anarchy being loosed upon the world. On all sides of us, and right here in our midst—a killing field.

Must this be? Must this world die, must all worlds? Must every-thing done become undone? Must every fabric unravel, every con-struction destruct, every integration disintegrate? Must every institution, social order, civilization? Must all that is, unbe? Must these warm and precious taper flames be all snuffed out, first and foremost this flickering light inside us?

Must this be? . . . the primal, primordial human question. The password question that identifies us as *Homo sapiens*—if we couldn't ask it we'd still be apes. Like a Sphinx it waits to ambush every sen-tient being that comes strolling down the human path. Sooner or later, in one form or another, it accosts us personally, and in fear or in hope, we must each confront it in solitude.

Toward the end of his sojourn down here, one human sen-tience, a.k.a. Ludwig van Beethoven, asked this very question in heartbreakingly beautiful tones that he himself could not hear: "*Muss es sein?*" Beethoven, the first great modern musical sensibility, the first truly alienated modern artist, the heroic rebel whose fate-defying, fist-shaking, deathbed lithograph so long was hung on so many timid bourgeois wallpapers. The truth, of course, was other-wise. Deaf and dying, utterly alone, alone with the Alone, he asked "our" question, our uniquely human question, the same ultimate spiritual question Christ had asked at Gethsemane, Gautama at Bodh Gaya, Arjuna at Kurukshetra, Job in the Land of Uz. And he received and transcribed into music the same ultimate spiritual reply: "*Es muss sein.*"

It must be. Or, more accurately, "It must be!" With an ! because this was not the *must be* of a broken spirit but rather the *must be* of a spiritual fruition—of realization, accordance, relaxation, and peace. An embrace of what is, a coital embrace of the answer that obviates the question, of the only Truth that can set us free. It must be because . . . it is! Because *It* is.

Because It is that It is. Because I am that I am. Because the
Godhead, the Real, the Tao of these ten thousand things–one of
which is human being and another of which is our own particular
sample of it—knows what It's about. Knows what It's doing even if
we ourselves do not. And this what-It's-doing is the only thing that
is done, that ever has been and ever will be done. Done beyond this
extraordinary talent to "do" with which It has seen fit to grace our
primate species, our ability to "conceive" and "create," to reason
and to speculate, to "resist" or to cooperate, and even to tinker
around a little inside the sandbox of our speck of the universe; this
unique spice that It has, for reasons of Its own, added to Its stan-
dard primatial recipe; this universe of action, in which everything is
forever busy doing something fitting. Galaxies act galactically, elec-
trons electronically, and ourselves more or less humanly. But when
these and the other 9,997 things do, It alone is the doer. Not just
because Its power overpowers them. Because there's no power but.
It's the only power there is.

> "How can we tell, Meister Eckhart, whether
> something that happens is according to the will of
> God?"
> "By the fact that it happens."

With this, Eckhart Zenji, that magnificent medieval, said it.
With this laser insight, the human psyche penetrates to the heart of
the human matter. We've drilled down to the adamantine bedrock
that upholds all our spiritual structures. Upon this rock every great
religion founds its faith and erects its church. Trust in the Is, in the
Is that Must Be, in the Ultimate Reality that is that Reality of
everything, this Reality of me.

When all is said and done—that is, when we ourselves have said
all we can say and done all we can do, when this poor exhausted self
of ours finally gives up on its "mission impossible" and collapses in
a heap—then at long last we can stop trying to thrash our way

through to some fantastic Elsewhere and perhaps, in the ensuing silence, we will be free to take our first real look at all that's right here. A clearer eye in us may be free to focus and we may, in the poet's phrase, "recognize the place for the first time." This place we live in, where our lives have come to life, as the place we belong.

To recognize reality, what here and now is, and to trust it. Here, in its essence, is the faith beyond the faiths, the rising of the sun that never ever sets, the arrival of a new religion that's been here from the start, a faith so old it looks like new, a timeless faith whose time has come. Up to now this has been the faith of the few—the "narrow way," confined to the esoteric elite, the so-called mystics of every religious tradition. "The world has many religions, the mystics have but one." Mystics, so called and inaccurately. For us, with all the new information that's been pouring in on us lately, with all the hard data we've been getting about the actual nature of things, the term *mysticism*, which "begins in *mist* and ends in *schism*"—has become obsolete. It's an anachronism these days, a misnomer. It's time we replaced it with a word that better reflects the facts.

My suggestion is *Realism*. Realism with a big R. A faith in nothing less than Reality Itself. Not that squint-eyed realism of the self-styled realists, the glaucomatous vision of that two-dimensional visual field. We've finally grown too smart for that, thank God. No, a whole Realism of the Whole Shebang, the Totality, which is the sum of all we know plus all we don't know. A wide-open vision that looks at everything and accepts everything, that denies nothing, that divides nothing, sections off nothing, segregates nothing, edits out nothing. In this faith beyond the faiths, which can be found above and beneath and within all traditional spiritualities, we've finally got ourselves an image of God worthy of creatures created in the image of God. An image beyond the images.

To be an Is of the Isness; to commend our spirits to the living Mystery of which we are part; to be at home in our home, this cosmos into which we were born and into which we are dying; to attune this small human instrument we're playing to the music of

the spheres—here is the ideal to which the faith beyond the faiths
aspires. Up there shines the Pole Star of a Realistic earthly journey,
up there the True North that enables us to navigate our ways down
here. All the rest follows.

And the rest—need I say it?—means work.

Work. What else? This system we find ourselves of is alive and
dynamic. The whole universe is on the move. And the system
works; it works beautifully. Everything in it is doing its job. Work is
the ever-changing way of that never-changing cosmos. Of this
human microcosmos too. Work is our life and work our joy—it is,
for as long as we're here as ego-bodied beings, anyhow. After this,
who knows? And before this, who remembers?

Work? But what precisely is human work? To see that, we have
to take a good look at ourselves as a species, the same kind of look
we've learned to take at other species, and recognize ourselves for
what we are.

Evolutionwise, we're obviously a transitional life-form, a currently rather unstable composite of top terrestrial animal plus
something more and else that tops that. A not-yet-homogenized
biological mix. As this biological mix, it's perfectly natural and normal for us to feel mixed up, to feel confused and cross-purposed to
a degree no lesser species does—or could. Given such genomic
givens, how could we possibly be otherwise? Still and nevertheless,
our atypical nature is natural, exactly as natural as any other form of
nature. It does *not* present a problem—nature hasn't got any problems. It only presents itself—in this instance to us. As a what is, in
the What Is, this is simply our fact to be dealt with. There's no reason to get anxious or guilty about what simply is. On the contrary,
nature, in showing us our own nature, is showing us our way. We
can't see ourselves without seeing our work.

What is our work? Work means directed application of energy.
Most of the work of the universe, in our view anyway, is done

THE FAITH BEYOND THE FAITHS

"unconsciously" by what we think is "insentient" being—electro-magnetic, thermonuclear, biochemical, and so on. This truth holds for us as well—we don't keep telling our hearts to pump or our enzymes to digest or our flesh to heal.

For sentient beings like us, work means to expend life-energy "consciously." For the animal-plus-something being of humans, work is clearly animal work plus something more and other. As of this writing, most human energy still must and does go into animal work. Animal work is the work of survival—which continues apace, even though no animal to date has ever succeeded in surviving. Survival starts from right here with ourself, ground zero of our impact into being, and ripples out in concentric waves from this epicenter into the environmental surround—to our nearest and dearest familiars, to our neighbor, our tribe, our nation, our race; to our species, to friendly species, to species in general; to our places on earth, to the earth itself, toward the infinite beyond. The animal work of survival is our true work, appropriate, fulfilling, and vital. Nature herself sounds our work call and we ignore it at our peril. Nevertheless and notwithstanding, this work is our animal work. It is not our human work.

ADULTHOOD

Our *human* work? We really should have a pretty good idea what that is by now, since our teachers everywhere have been tell-ing us for ages. In the ancient East, the departing Buddha enjoined us to "hold fast to the Truth as a refuge and work out your salvation with diligence." In the modern West, a zaddik reminded us, "You didn't begin the work, you won't finish the work, but who gave you permission to stop working?" Both were talking about the same work, our human work.

Our human work is to partake in our own evolution. As a species we've matured to adolescence, on the very brink of our adulthood. As a species we are manifesting the typical traits of adolescence. In cultures around the globe we see them: the restless dissatisfaction with old forms that served well enough before but that now have lost their relevance; the inability to believe in physical and metaphysical explanations that no longer explain, in categorical boundaries that are now overrun, in descriptions of a reality past that have ceased to describe reality present; the disillusionment with spiritualities from which the spirit has departed.

Adolescence gives all species a difficult time of it, and our own most of all. We're a lot more certain about the wrong of what's old than about the right of what's new. Yet the way of rejection also lies along the spiritual path, the *via negativa*, the way of Neti, Neti, of "not this and not this." In any event, there's no turning back now. To regress and retreat toward childhood is to invite insanity, as our century has amply demonstrated, for both individuals and societies. The only way through is the way ahead—to our adulthood.

Human adults are people who can be entrusted with responsibility, who don't need a policeman to keep them from criminality or a clergyman to herd them to spiritual water holes. The faith beyond the faiths means that we accept responsibility for our further evolution. And at the point of human adulthood, evolution moves inward. Interior evolution is spiritual. The mutational process continues. We keep changing outwardly, but it's a changing from within. As in seed to root to sprout to plant to flower to fruit to seed, the forms transform but the quintessence remains. It is, simply and literally, what is meant by that paradoxical "mystical" phrase, "We become who we are."

The faith beyond the faiths is the religion of mature humanity. As observers have observed, every religious tradition contains two religions: one for its children and quite another for its grown-ups. As on the physical plane, the children of whatever faith have more in common with one another than they do with the grown-ups of their own faith. Joseph Campbell once offended Christians by calling Christianity a fine religion—for children. He could have, and probably would have, said the same thing about Buddhism, or Islam, Judaism, Hinduism and the rest. The real distinction is simply this: In spiritual childhood, we seek to focus God's attention onto us; in spiritual adulthood, we seek to focus our attention onto God.

As of this writing at the closing days of the second millennium A.D., there are obviously still far more children than adults among us. But our median age is rising.

BIBLIOGRAPHY

Anonymous. "The Cloud of Unknowing." In *Book of Privy Counsel* by the Medieval Mystics of England, edited by Eric Colledge. New York: Scribner's Sons, 1961.

Aquinas, Thomas. *A Shorter Summa: The Most Essential Philosophical Passages of St. Thomas Aquinas' Summa Theologica*. Edited by Peter J. Kreeft. San Francisco: Ignatius Press, 1993.

——. *Summa Theologica: A Concise Translation*. Translated by Timothy McDermott. Westminster, Md.: Christian Classics, 1989.

Armstrong, Karen. *A History of God*. New York: Knopf, 1993.

——. *Visions of God*. New York: Bantam Books, 1994.

Blackstone, Judith. *The Subtle Self: Personal Growth and Spiritual Practice*. (This book includes exercises in the Subtle Self Work. Available from the author.)

——. *Spiritual Transcendence and the Sense of Self* (forthcoming.)

Blake, William. "Auguries of Innocence." In *William Blake: The Complete Poems*, edited by Alicia Ostriker. New York: Schocken Books, 1969.

Bruteau, Beatrice. *Easter Mysteries*. New York: Crossroad, 1995.

——. *Radical Optimism*. New York: Crossroad, 1993.

——. *What We Can Learn from the East*. New York: Crossroad, 1995.

Buber, Martin. *I and Thou*. Translated by Ronald Gregor Smith. New York: Charles Scribner's Sons, 1958.

——. *Between Man and Man*. New York: Macmillan, 1966.

——. *Tales of the Hasidim: The Later Masters*. New York: Schocken Books, 1948.

Butterfield, Stephen T. *The Double Mirror: A Skeptical Journey into Buddhist Tantra.* Berkeley, Calif.: North Atlantic Books, 1994.

Course in Miracles. Chicago: Foundation for Inner Peace, 1985.

de Salzmann, Michel. "Footnote to the Gurdjieff Literature." In *Gurdjieff: An Annotated Bibliography.* New York: Garland Publishing, 1985.

Eck, Diana. *Encountering God: A Spiritual Journey from Bozeman to Banaras.* Boston: Beacon Press, 1993.

Eliot, T. S. "Little Giddings" and "East Coker." *Four Quartets.* New York: Harcourt Brace Jovanovich, 1971.

Finley, James. *Merton's Palace of Nowhere.* Notre Dame, Ind.: Ave Maria Press, 1992.

Fox, Matthew. *Wrestling with the Prophets.* San Francisco: Harper, 1995.

Frankel, Estelle. *Tikkun* 9, no. 5 (Sept.–Oct., 1994).

Gillman, Neil. *Sacred Fragments: Recovering Theology for the Modern Jew.* New York: The Jewish Publication Society, 1990.

Glatzer, Nahum N. *Franz Rosenzweig: His Life and Thought.* New York: Shocken Books, 1961.

Goldberg, Natalie. *Long Quiet Highway: Waking Up in America.* New York: Bantam Books, 1993.

Gurdjieff, G. I. *Beelzebub's Tales to His Grandson.* New York: E. P. Dutton, 1964. Examples of Gurdjieff movements can be seen in the film *Meetings with Remarkable Men*, Corinth Video, 1987.

Harvey, Andrew. *The Way of Passion: A Celebration of Rumi.* Berkeley, Calif.: Frog, Ltd., 1994.

Heidegger, Martin. *Being and Time.* New York: Harper & Row, 1962.

Heschel, Abraham Joshua. *God in Search of Man: A Philosophy of Judaism.* New York: Farrar, Straus and Giroux, 1995.

——. *Man Is Not Alone: A Philosophy of Religion.* New York: Farrar, Straus and Giroux, 1994.

Hopkins, Gerard Manley. *Poems and Prose of Gerard Manley Hopkins.* New York: Penguin Books, 1963.

Kaplan, Aryeh. *Jewish Meditation: A Practical Guide.* New York: Schocken Books, 1985.

Kaufman, William E. *Journeys: An Introductory Guide to Jewish Mysticism.* New York: Bloch Publishing Co., 1980.

Kierkegaard, Søren. *Purity of Heart.* Translated by Douglas V. Steere. New York: Harper, 1948.

Kornfield, Jack. *A Path with Heart: A Guide Through the Perils and Promises of Spiritual Life.* New York: Bantam Books, 1993.

Kushner, Harold S. *To Life! A Celebration of Jewish Being and Thinking.* Boston: Warner Books, 1993.

Loori, John Daido. *Two Arrows Meeting in Mid-Air.* Boston: Charles E. Tuttle Co., Inc., 1994.

Maimonides, Moses. *Guide to the Perplexed.* Translated by Shlomo Pines. Chicago: University of Chicago Press, 1974.

Marcel, Gabriel. *Creative Fidelity.* Translated by Robert Rosthal. New York: Farrar Straus, 1964.

——. *Metaphysical Journal.* Chicago: Gateway, 1952.

——. *The Mystery of Being.* Chicago: Gateway, 1960.

McCorkle, Beth. *The Gurdjieff Years 1929–1949: Recollections of Louise March.* Walworth, N.Y.: The Work Study Association, 1990.

BIBLIOGRAPHY

Merrell-Wolff, Franklin. *The Philosophy of Consciousness Without an Object.* New York: Julian Press, 1973.

Merton, Thomas. *The Asian Journals of Thomas Merton.* New York: New Direction Books, 1975.

——. *New Seeds of Contemplation.* New York: New Directions, 1961.

Millay, Edna St. Vincent. *Collected Poems.* New York: Harper, 1949.

Miller, Ronald H. *Dialogue and Disagreement: Franz Rosenzweig's Relevance to Contemporary Jewish-Christian Understanding.* Lanham, Md.: University Press of America, 1989.

Moore, Thomas. *Care of the Soul.* New York: HarperCollins Publishers, 1994.

——. *Meditations: On the Monk Who Dwells in Daily Life.* New York: HarperCollins Publishers, 1994.

O'Halloran, Maura. *Pure Heart, Enlightened Mind.* Boston: Charles E. Tuttle Co., Inc., 1994.

Otto, Rudolf. *The Idea of the Holy.* London: Oxford University Press, 1981.

Pirsig, Robert M. *Zen and the Art of Motorcycle Maintenance.* New York: William Morrow, 1974.

Plaut, Gunther W., ed. *The Torah: A Modern Commentary.* New York: Union of American Hebrew Congregations, 1981.

Pourrat, P. "La Spiritualité Chretienne." Quoted in *Staretz Amvrosy* by John B. Dunlop. Belmont, Mass.: Nordland, 1972.

Rosenzweig, Franz. *The Star of Redemption.* Translated by William W. Hallo. Boston: Beacon Press, 1964.

Saint Benedict. *The Rule of St. Benedict.* Edited by Timothy Fry. Collegeville, Minn.: The Liturgical Press, 1981.

Salinger, J. D. *Franny and Zooey*. Boston: Little, Brown, 1961.

Schleiermacher, Friedrich. *On Religion: Speeches to Its Cultured Despisers*. Cambridge, England: Cambridge University Press, 1992.

Segal, William. *The Ten Oxherding Pictures*. Vt.: Green River Press, 1988.

Shapiro, Rami. *Why on This Night? A Pesach Haggadah*. Miami, Fla.: Temple Beth Or, 1993.

Shulevitz, Uri. *The Treasure*. New York: Farrar, Straus, Giroux, 1978.

Telushkin, Joseph. *Jewish Literacy: The Most Important Things to Know About the Jewish Religion, Its People, and Its History*. New York: William Morrow, 1991.

Thich Nhat Hanh. *Being Peace*. Berkeley, Calif.: Parallax Press, 1987.

———. *Peace Is Every Step*. New York: Bantam Books, 1992.

———. *The Diamond that Cuts Through Illusion*. Berkeley, Calif.: Parallax Press, 1992.

Tikkun: a Bi-monthly Jewish Critique of Politics, Culture, and Society. New York.

Tillich, Paul. *Systematic Theology*. Chicago: University of Chicago Press, 1967.

Trungpa, Chögyam. *Cutting Through Spiritual Materialism*. Berkeley, Calif.: Shambhala Publications, 1973.

Twersky, Isadore. *A Maimonides Reader*. New York: Behrman House, 1972.

Tworkov, Helen. "Life with a Capital L, An Interview with Philip Kapleau Roshi." *Tricycle: The Buddhist Review*, vol. 2, no. 4, summer 1993. New York.

———. "Interbeing with Thich Nhat Hanh: An Interview." *Tricycle: The Buddhist Review*, vol. 4, no. 4, summer 1995. New York.

The Urantia Book. Chicago: The Urantia Foundation, 1955.

von Brück, Michael. *The Unity of Reality*. New York: Paulist Press, 1991.

Walters, John. *The Essence of Buddhism*. New York: Thos. Crowell, 1961.

Waskow, Arthur. "Facing the Pharaohs." *New Menorah, The Journal of ALEPH: Alliance for Jewish Renewal*, no. 39 (spring 1995).

Wolpe, David. *In Speech and in Silence: The Jewish Quest for God*. New York: Henry Holt, 1992.

ABOUT THE AUTHORS

Laura Bernstein

Laura Bernstein has an M.S.W. degree from the University of Chicago, and is a graduate of the Child Therapy Program of the Institute for Psychoanalysis. She studied Buddhism at the Chicago Shambhala Center. She is, at this time, a rabbinical student at the Hebrew Seminary of the Deaf. She receives mail at 339 Lakeside Place, Highland Park, IL 60035.

Judith Blackstone

Judith Blackstone developed Subtle Self Work, an approach to realizing fundamental consciousness. She is codirector of the Realization Center in Woodstock, New York, and also teaches in New York City, Burlington, Vermont, Marin County, California, and at the Esalen Institute. Her training was in Buddhism, Vedanta, psychology, and dance. She receives mail at Box 1209, Woodstock, NY 12498. Her voice-mail number is 914-334-2401.

Beatrice Bruteau

Beatrice Bruteau has a doctorate in philosophy from Fordham University. Her religious background is in Vedanta and Catholicism. She is a teacher, speaker, and writer. She is the founder of the Schola Contemplationis, a network community for contemplatives of all traditions. She is also the founder and guide of the Fellowship of the Holy Trinity, an ecumenical nonresidential monastic community for men and women, based on the Rule of St. Benedict and its own Rule. She receives mail at 3425 Forest Lane, Pfafftown, NC 27040.

Robert Granat

Robert Granat is a prize-winning writer of short stories, novels, essays, and reviews. He is a subsistence farmer. He and his wife have been serving the local communities of northern New Mexico in many capacities since 1950. Granat receives mail at Box 475, Alcalde, NM 87511.

Annabeth McCorkle

Annabeth McCorkle is a writer. She has been connected, as both a student and a guide, with the Gurdjieff tradition of inner work for more than thirty years. Her voice-mail number is 716-223-0337. Her E-mail address is YPTR61A@Prodigy.com.

Ronald H. Miller

Ron Miller has degrees in classics, philosophy, and theology and has taught in high schools and colleges. After leaving the Jesuits, he received a Ph.D. in comparative religions from Northwestern University. He is a founder and codirector of Common Ground, a center for interfaith study and dialogue, where he also teaches. He is currently chair of the Religion Department at Lake Forest College. Miller receives mail at Lake Forest College, Lake Forest, IL, 60045. His E-mail address is rmiller@lfmail.lfc.edu.

Lorette Zirker

Lorette Zirker is a writer of essays and editor of books, and has been a columnist and reporter. She is a lay-ordained, continuing student of Zen Buddhism. Zirker receives mail at Box 249, High Rolls, NM 88325.

A NOTE ON THE TYPE

The text of this book is typeset in a digitized version of the typeface Janson. The original version of Janson was long believed to have been created by the Dutchman Anton Janson, who was a practicing type founder in Leipzig during the years 1668–1687. It is now thought, however, that the typeface is actually the work of Nicholas Kis (1650–1702), a Hungarian, who most probably learned his trade from the master Dutch type founder Dirk Voskens. Kis was born in 1650, pursued theological studies, and obtained a reputation as a Greek and Latin scholar. He became an internationally recognized type cutter during his years of apprenticeship and work in Amsterdam, and was in great demand as a type cutter of "exotic" alphabets.